Knowledge Management in the Pharmaceutical Industry

Reviews for
Knowledge Management in the Pharmaceutical Industry

'This book demonstrates the critical importance of knowledge management and data sharing to translate the new vision of drug development into concrete actions. This is a timely endeavor since more than ever therapeutic advances depend on integrative analysis of big data by scientists acquainted to the principles of collective intelligence.'

Michel Goldman, Executive Director, Innovative Medicines Initiative (IMI)

'This isn't just a book describing the theory of knowledge management, but rather an illustration of how it can be applied to the real, challenging world of the pharmaceutical industry. For those attempting to improve ways of working collaboratively in pharma, look here for some practical and pre-tested ideas, even if a formal KM strategy is already in place.'

Alison Zartarian, AstraZeneca

'With little published in this area, this book provides valuable, concrete evidence of the value of Knowledge Management (KM) to Pharma operations. Key KM principles are exemplified by a blend of case material and anecdote – easy to read and tempting to adopt. The content should stimulate readers to seek the KM opportunities in their own organisations – in Pharma and beyond.'

Sandra Ward, Principal Consultant, Beaworthy Consulting

Knowledge Management in the Pharmaceutical Industry

Enhancing Research, Development and Manufacturing Performance

ELISABETH GOODMAN and JOHN RIDDELL

Routledge
Taylor & Francis Group

LONDON AND NEW YORK

First published in paperback 2024

First published 2014 by Gower Publishing

Published 2016 by Routledge
4 Park Square, Milton Park, Abingdon, Oxon OX14 4RN

and by Routledge
605 Third Avenue, New York, NY 10158

Routledge is an imprint of the Taylor & Francis Group, an informa business

Publisher's Note
The publisher has gone to great lengths to ensure the quality of this reprint but points out that some imperfections in the original copies may be apparent.

British Library Cataloguing in Publication Data
A catalogue record for this book is available from the British Library

Library of Congress Cataloging-in-Publication Data
Goodman, E. C. (Elisabeth C.)
  Knowledge management in the pharmaceutical industry : enhancing research, development and manufacturing performance / by Elisabeth Goodman and John Riddell.
    pages cm
  Includes bibliographical references and index.
  ISBN 978-1-4094-5335-2 (hardback) -- ISBN 978-1-4094-5336-9 (ebook) -- ISBN 978-1-4724-0805-1 (epub) 1. Pharmaceutical industry--Management. 2. Knowledge management. 3. Research, Industrial. I. Title.
  HD9665.5.G66 2014
  615.1068'4--dc23

                                                                                    2014012868

ISBN: 978-1-4094-5335-2 (hbk)
ISBN: 978-1-03-283742-0 (pbk)
ISBN: 978-1-315-59118-6 (ebk)

DOI: 10.4324/9781315591186

Contents

List of Figures

List of Tables

About the Authors

Elisabeth Goodman is the Owner and Principal Consultant of RiverRhee Consulting, whose primary aim is to enhance team effectiveness. Knowledge Management is one of the four main approaches used to achieve this. Elisabeth has 25 years' experience in Pharmaceutical Research and Development (R&D), where she has held management roles in Information and Library Management, and internal training and consultancy roles supporting business teams on a global basis. In the 1990s she co-led SmithKline Beecham's Information Management department's efforts to introduce an organisational Knowledge Management strategy. In 2001 she joined an internal GSK business consulting team to foster knowledge working practices within the team and the wider organisation. Elisabeth is the author of several articles, book chapters and presentations on Knowledge Management. She has a BSc in Biochemistry, an MSc in Information Science and is also an experienced and certified practitioner in change management, Lean Six Sigma, Myers Briggs Type Indicator (MBTI), and a registered and approved Growth Coach and Leadership and Management Trainer for GrowthAccelerator.

John Riddell has a BSc in Chemistry and over 30 years' experience of working in pharmaceutical production where he has held technical, operational and project management roles working with both small and large teams from a local to a global basis. For nine years John played a key role in the GlaxoSmithKline Manufacturing Knowledge Management programme spread across 80 manufacturing locations globally, from its inception through to it being embedded in manufacturing operations. He was responsible for a wide range of activities including leading the communities of practice programme, managing the expertise location system, developing knowledge transfer techniques and the training of local knowledge managers as change agents. John has Associate status with RiverRhee Consulting and Knoco, is a certified practitioner in Lean Six Sigma and is a Member of the Association for Project Management.

Foreword

PROFESSOR JACKIE HUNTER, CBE

In recent years the Pharmaceutical Industry has undergone, and continues to undergo, unprecedented restructuring and changes in many of its areas including R&D, Manufacturing, Supply Chain Logistics and Commercial activities.

R&D is at the forefront of these changes. The Pharmaceutical Industry's lifeblood is innovation – without innovative pipelines, companies struggle to survive – indeed thin pipelines have been the driver for the many mergers and acquisitions in the industry over the past two decades. The source of innovation for the industry is also changing – with the boundaries between pharmaceutical companies and between commercial organisations and academia becoming more fluid. At the same time the costs of R&D have escalated – the industry needs to either find ways to increase its chances of success, decrease risk or seek to reduce the cost of failure in order for it to be sustainable in the future. External sources of innovation (academia, biotechnology companies) now deliver a large proportion of pharmaceutical companies' R&D pipelines. Companies are operating globally across the whole value chain and the need to share information and knowledge across time zones, continents and cultures provides further challenges.

With these changes the need for Knowledge Management to be more widely used and integrated becomes critical. In the past companies have continued to duplicate target validation activities, have not shared the learnings from unsuccessful clinical trials and generally been protective of all their data. This is no longer tenable from both a financial and social perspective – transparency is an ever increasing requirement from key stakeholders such as the regulators and patients. As mentioned in this book, this protection of data also extended internally in the past with a general reluctance of people across an organisation to share information and knowledge. An additional factor is the loss of the tacit knowledge residing in departing employees which has particular relevance for the Pharmaceutical Industry.

In addition, the rate at which biomedical data is accumulating is growing exponentially. How that data is harnessed and shared depends on the systems, processes and culture that form the framework of Knowledge Management. The linking of data with the right people creates the knowledge, both explicit and tacit, that is essential for innovation. Nowhere is this more crucial than in the Pharmaceutical Industry.

It is vitally important for companies to develop a holistic, integrated and company-wide Knowledge Management strategy – indeed it is hard to see how any pharmaceutical company will be competitive in the future without one. This book is therefore very timely.

The authors provide a general overview of Knowledge Management, before discussing it in relation to the Pharmaceutical Industry. Importantly they have used real-life examples, gained through their own experience and interviews with industry experts, to illustrate some of the best practices (and pitfalls) in implementing effective Knowledge Management. They highlight the importance of articulating the benefits of such a strategy and describe the key enablers for effective Knowledge Management. For anyone embarking on developing and implementing Knowledge Management strategies in biomedical science within and without the Pharmaceutical Industry, especially in the context of the new Open Innovation agenda, this book will prove invaluable.

****

Professor Jacqueline Hunter CBE, is currently Chief Executive of OI Pharma Partners Limited. She has an extensive record in developing and running global centres of excellence in pharmaceutical research and is a leader in the application of Open Innovation principles to Life Sciences R&D. In 2010 Professor Hunter received a CBE for Services to the Pharmaceutical Industry and was presented with a Women of Achievement in Science, Engineering & Technology award. She is a Fellow of the British Pharmacological Society and holds a personal Chair at St George's Hospital Medical School.

Preface

The principles and approaches inherent to Knowledge Management are something that we both live and breathe by! They have been intrinsic to our work in the Pharmaceutical Industry, and continue to be something that we encourage and support our clients in as part of our work as independent consultants. They are also an underlying theme in our writing, seminars and workshops. In fact it was as a result of Elisabeth's blogs on the subject that we were invited to write this book. We believe that the connection between Knowledge Management and the Pharmaceutical Industry is both necessary and strong during this time of significant change in the industry. Our approach has been to combine our own experience and insights with those of a cross section of pharmaceutical professionals and Knowledge Management practitioners. We have captured these external inputs through informal interviews and represented them in the form of case studies and quotes.

We hope that you find this book an informative and pragmatic as well as an inspiring read.

PART I
Pharmaceutical Knowledge Management

Chapter 1
Setting the Parameters

Introduction

Knowledge Management (KM) is notoriously difficult to define and indeed represents different things to different people. There is no set formula: every company has its own structure, environment, culture and goals, all of which have a critical effect on KM. Every approach and application is unique: there is definitely no 'one size fits all'. This is perhaps why the concept has struggled for wider recognition: it is open to interpretation, represents different things to different people and requires a deep understanding (along with some passion!) for it to be successfully initiated and embedded within an organisation.

In this opening chapter, we provide a comprehensive coverage of the discipline for those who are relatively new to it. We begin with a brief look at the origins of KM, discuss some principles and definitions, and why we should be doing it at all. We also introduce our KM Framework to help pull all of this together, and provide a selection of Good Practices along with some of our insights and further references for those who would like to find out more.

An Introduction to Knowledge Management

THE ROOTS AND DEVELOPMENT OF KNOWLEDGE MANAGEMENT

The social practice of Knowledge Transfer has been around since cavemen started hunting in groups and painting their experience on cave walls. Knowledge Management as a business practice has been developing since the 1990s. Koenig (*What is KM? Knowledge Management Explained* May 2012) attributes the birth of KM to the use of intranets in large global consultancies, where people recognised that if they shared their knowledge about their clients and about how they went about their work they could avoid reinventing the wheel, underbid their competitors, and make more profit. They then realised that they also had a product in Knowledge Management.

One can argue that the key principles of Knowledge Management were established in the 1990s, and that in the 'Noughties' KM has developed through:

- new computer-based technologies;

- a deeper exploration of methodologies and approaches by established experts and practitioners;

- the education and up-skilling of new practitioners;

- absorption into, or combination with other business management disciplines such as information and library management, records management, Data Management, organisational learning, business and process improvement, and so on.

WHAT DO WE MEAN BY KNOWLEDGE MANAGEMENT?

Some regard it as 'old hat' but we believe it is useful to describe data, information and knowledge as a hierarchy.

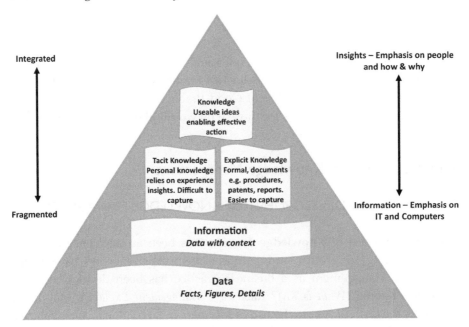

Figure 1.1   Knowledge, information and data

Some also add a further layer, wisdom, to cover the choices and judgments that people make with their new knowledge, but we will contain our description to the three layers. It helps to explain the hierarchy by using the analogy of a train journey:

- data: departure and arrival times as given in the timetable;

- information: the additional content that enhances the data such as whether the train has first class carriages and a buffet car;

- explicit knowledge: it may be that the train is delayed by x minutes, or that only the front carriages will stop at a particular station. This will be provided on the display board at the station, or announced over the public address system;

- tacit knowledge: where regular travelers on this train stand on the platform to access the doors. A fellow passenger tells you that this train is always ten minutes late!

Here are a few definitions to help create a more detailed representation of Knowledge Management. We begin with Duhon's from the relatively early days of KM:

> *Knowledge Management is a discipline that promotes an integrated approach to identifying, capturing, evaluating, retrieving, and sharing all of an enterprise's information assets. These assets may include databases, documents, policies, procedures, and previously un-captured expertise and experience in individual workers. (Duhon 1998)*

The first part of Duhon's definition has a clear connection with the cycle of knowledge that we favour and describe below, but it stops short of mentioning knowledge sharing and does not cover how the 'information assets' must be used to justify the whole process and to gain value and benefit.

The second part of Duhon's definition leads us into the area of explicit and tacit knowledge. Not everyone buys into the use of these terms:

> *Nonaka and Takeuchi's linguistic confusion that led to the false dichotomy of tacit and explicit knowledge. (Newman 2002)*

However, we believe that they help to provide a context for applying Knowledge Management tools and techniques and are implicit in an understanding of KM itself. Defining explicit and tacit knowledge helps us to think more clearly about the processes that we apply to knowledge in order to derive benefit:

- Explicit knowledge is what is written or recorded in documents, databases, websites and so on. It is very tangible and can be easily stored, accessed, worked on, and transmitted or distributed.

- Tacit knowledge is the knowledge that is in our heads such as know-how, experience, insights, ideas and intuition. It is usually richer knowledge but can be difficult to define and access. It requires the right environment, culture and questioning techniques to unlock and share it.

The flow between tacit and explicit knowledge is as follows (Figure 1.2):

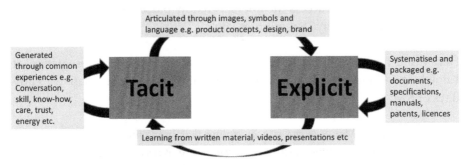

Figure 1.2   Tacit and explicit knowledge

This dynamic between tacit and explicit knowledge is also intrinsic to the Knowledge Transfer processes that we describe later in this chapter.

If we fast forward to close to the present day, Snowden's definition is an example of how the thinking about Knowledge Management has shifted:

The purpose of Knowledge Management is to provide support for improved decision making and innovation throughout the organization. This is achieved through the effective management of human intuition and experience augmented by the provision of information, processes and technology together with training and mentoring programmes.

The following guiding principles will be applied:

- *all projects will be clearly linked to operational and strategic goals*
- *as far as possible the approach adopted will be to stimulate local activity rather than impose central solutions*
- *co-ordination and distribution of learning will focus on allowing adaptation of good practice to the local context*
- *management of the KM function will be based on a small centralized core, with a wider distributed network. (Snowden 2009)*

There is much more of an emphasis here on tacit knowledge, on the practical application or outcomes of KM, the importance of relating it to business goals, and the desire to make it as decentralised and so embedded into day-to-day work as possible. It makes a shift from the process and means to the outcomes achieved by KM. We believe that this is the fundamental place to focus on as we shall discuss later.

The last definition is Gurteen's, and although ten years older than Snowden's, it is the one that's very close to our own current vision of KM:

Knowledge Management is a business philosophy. It is an emerging set of principles, processes, organisational structures, and technology applications that help people share and leverage their knowledge to meet their business objectives. (Gurteen 1999)

Gurteen refers to Knowledge Management both as a philosophy for business (a way of thinking) and a means to achieving business objectives (the processes). His definition also neatly links together the triangle of people, processes and technology which are critical to KM, and which we reflect in our knowledge framework below. The only difference from the present is that the principles are no longer emerging but are very much established.

A Framework for Knowledge Management

There are many aspects to Knowledge Management, and our framework attempts to pull these together in order to provide a 'helicopter view' or reference model for this book.

A Framework for Knowledge Management

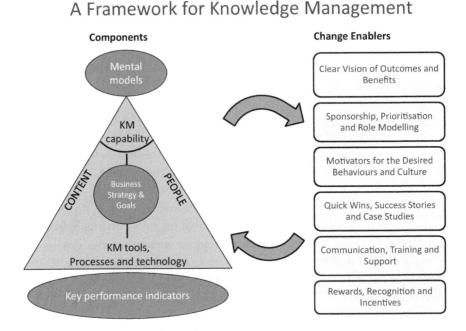

Figure 1.3   A framework for Knowledge Management

The left hand side of the framework consists of what we believe are the core components of Knowledge Management: the mental models that provide the common language around KM in the organisation, the business goals that provide the context for KM activities, and the measures (or Key Performance Indicators – KPIs) that determine their success, the sources of knowledge (Content Management and people), and the tools, processes, technology and capabilities that facilitate their flow.

The right hand side of the framework consists of the change enablers. As the name implies they are the key to influencing mindsets, values, behaviours and ways of working within the organisation. They help people to 'really get it'. This shift can be driven by a belief that Knowledge Management is 'the right thing to do'. But a more sustainable driver is the role modelling by managers and executives who themselves 'get it'.

This chapter focuses on the components of our Knowledge Management Framework (KM Framework), the left hand side. We come back to the change enablers in Chapter 7 where we explore strategies for driving and sustaining KM in the Pharmaceutical Industry, and our interviewees' experience of putting them into practice.

Mental models, a tie in to the organisation's strategy and goals, and KPIs provide the 'scaffolding' for our KM Framework, so we begin with these three.

MENTAL MODELS

Mental models provide people with a way of thinking about Knowledge Management: the common language that can be used within an organisation. There are two such models that are at the heart of KM: the 'Knowledge Cycle', and 'Learning Before, During and After'.

THE KNOWLEDGE CYCLE

The Knowledge Cycle is a representation of the various stages of knowledge development and use.

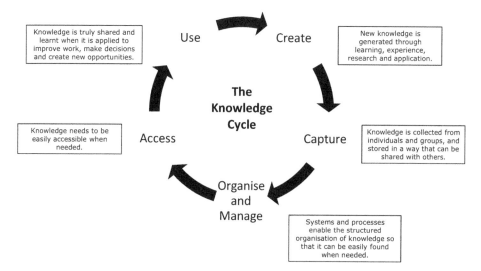

Figure 1.4   The Knowledge Cycle

This model is circular: the usual starting point is the creation of knowledge and its application to an activity that will in turn create new knowledge.

It is easy to apply the model to explicit knowledge, but it also works for tacit knowledge if we think of the brain as the central organising and managing function rather than some form of database or document. 'Capture' then represents listening and learning, and 'Access' is the dialogue involved in asking and answering questions.

It is also helpful to think about the model in reverse, that is, if you want to 'Use' knowledge then you need to be able to 'Access' it. Effective 'Access' requires effective 'Organisation and Management' and so on back round the cycle to 'Create'. This mental model therefore helps to set the context for effective systems and processes.

The right hand side of the cycle is predominantly a *push* process: pushing the knowledge out so that it can be available. The left hand side is a *pull* process: seeking out the necessary knowledge.

Finally, although the 'Create', 'Capture', 'Access' and 'Use' stages require systems and processes to help them function, they are predominantly cultural challenges: they are about getting people to work in a different way. The 'Organise' stage usually requires some additional investment which can often be neglected or ignored. Information Technology investment may be required to provide a knowledge base that can be widely accessed, and personnel required to establish processes, provide training, manage the lifecycle of content or facilitate knowledge sharing. The availability of these resources and the achievement of the cultural change will again depend on the change enablers that we explore further in Chapter 7.

LEARN BEFORE, DURING AND AFTER

If the Knowledge Cycle provides the 'what' for Knowledge Management, there is another approach that provides the 'when'. The approach developed by BP of 'Learn Before', 'Learn During' and 'Learn After', described in *Learning to Fly* (Collison and Parcell 2004), is central to almost every Knowledge Management practitioner's approach that we have come across. Collison and Parcell represent these three steps in the form of a continuous loop, which closely matches the Knowledge Cycle. Learn Before mirrors the left hand side of the circle, that is, 'Access' and 'Use'. Learn After echoes the right hand side of the circle, that is, 'Create' and 'Capture'. Learn During embodies the whole cycle.

The Learn Before, During and After mental model reinforces the message that Knowledge Management is at the core of our work. It is also a good prompt for project managers, or anyone starting a new task or activity. They can ask themselves the question: 'Before I start, what can I "learn before" from others who have done something similar?' And the same applies for Learn During and Learn After, although in those cases they would also be asking themselves the question: 'What have I learnt that I could usefully share with others?' With this approach, people can look for and be given the appropriate 'just in time' tools, training and support that they need, and perhaps be given support through implementation. This is a better approach than to go through training in a number of tools, only to have forgotten about them, or forgotten how to apply them, when the time comes. We describe the techniques associated with Learn Before, During and After in Chapter 2.

Linking Knowledge Management to Business Strategy and Goals

Any serious attempt at Knowledge Management requires resources, effort and commitment. These can only be obtained if senior management is committed to supporting KM, and this commitment is best gained and demonstrated when Knowledge Management initiatives are aligned with the business strategy and play a key role in delivering its goals and objectives.

According to O'Dell (O'Dell, _The Executive's Role in Knowledge Management_ 2004), typical business objectives from which a business case for a KM initiative might be developed include:

- improved quality of products and services;

- building on lessons learned and shortening the learning curve;

- increased profitability;

- lower operating costs;

- innovation;

- re-use of past designs and experiences.

Clear business objectives such as these act as the basis for identifying what knowledge the organisation currently has to support its objectives, what knowledge it needs, and how it might go about addressing any gaps in a way that can be sustained. The business may also have some specific issues that it needs to address in which Knowledge Management tools or processes can play a role. Typical examples include:

- The business is concerned about a wave of retirees, or the potential loss of key people to competitors, with a consequent significant loss of knowledge. In this case a Knowledge Retention programme might help.

- Operational efficiencies are low or variable across an organisation. There is a potential to learn from each other and the facilitation of Best Practice transfer would help this.

- The business suffers from repeated failures in a particular area, implying that learnings are not being identified or are being forgotten. After Action or Learning Reviews can identify remedial action and improvement of internal processes.

A focus on the contribution of KM to the achievement of business objectives, combined with quantitative or qualitative measurement of the impact of related initiatives (KPIs), will make results more visible and help to foster the new behaviours and ways of working required to encourage and sustain change.

Key Performance Indicators (KPIs)

The measurement of the performance of some areas of business is relatively straightforward: sales revenue or volume, production output, number of enquiries generated, are all easily measured and have a direct impact on the business. Since Knowledge Management is very much an enabler for effective working it is often hard to directly connect a KM activity to the bottom line, let alone attribute the benefit it has had in accounting terms.

The challenges involved can be illustrated, for example, when measuring the impact of sharing a Good Practice. The 'receiver' is likely to adapt the Good Practice to their own environment and put in the resources to make the change or improvement. It then makes most sense to allocate any cost benefit achieved to their local budget, rather than to some 'central pot'. However, if a central Knowledge Management 'office' is responsible for initiating the sharing of Good Practices, they may want an empirical central record of these kinds of local savings in order to demonstrate the impact of the overall programme. This requires careful management to avoid financial confusion, and of course sometimes by the time a benefit has been achieved how it actually came about may have been forgotten!

Collecting the right kind of measures is crucial to achieve and maintain support for Knowledge Management programmes. If senior managers do not see that KM is making a contribution to business success, they may de-prioritise it, reduce activities, reassign resources and ultimately discontinue the programme. Similarly, staff will be less likely to change the way they work if they do not perceive tangible benefits to their work, and visible examples of KM becoming the way the organisation 'does business'.

However, the tangible (outcome or 'lag') results of a KM programme can take a while to come through, and so some early (in-process, interim or 'lead') measures or metrics are required. The American Productivity and Quality Center (APQC) has carried out a lot of research in this area (O'Dell 2004) which we have adapted under three main headings.

1.   *Use the Organisation's Measures of Success as the Starting Point.* Instead of creating separate Knowledge Management measures of outcomes, develop measures that relate to the business outcomes that the KM activities are supporting. For example, the impact of the transfer of knowledge that enables an existing process to start up in a new location would be measured in terms of the difference between the timescale the business unit might have expected working in isolation, and that which was achieved.

2.   *Define Specific Measures for Specific KM Interventions.* For example, the cost and impact of a CoP will be measured differently from those of a Content Management system.

3.   *Select Metrics to Reflect Activity that Relates to the Business Outcome.* Many indicators of activity are available, and such metrics can be used during the early stages of a KM programme, or at the start of a new phase, to demonstrate to sponsors that an initiative is going in the right direction. Examples of such metrics include:
      – the number of documents added to a collaborative workspace – this is an in-process or interim measure;
      – the number of times documents are accessed – this is closer to an outcome measure as it shows that some use is being made of the documents, although it does not measure the benefit gained as a result;
      – the trend in the number of hits on a website – an upward trend over a period of time indicates that some value is being gained from the site as the same people are using it more, or more people are using it.

Combining these output measures and performance metrics into a set of KPIs should demonstrate progress with the KM programme. It will also help to identify issues and enable any remedial action to be taken.

Chapter 2
Relating People and Content

As we mentioned in Chapter 1, different people have different perspectives of what Knowledge Management is all about. Some people focus on managing knowledge as a resource (often closely coupled with Information Technology, Data Management, Document Management, Library and Information Management), others focus on learning, the sharing of knowledge and the stimulation of new ideas or innovation (closely linked with Human Resources, Training and Development). In our framework, we have called these two perspectives 'Content Management' and 'People' respectively. Together they provide the sources of knowledge available to the organisation.

Content Management

In Chapter 1 we described the knowledge, information and data hierarchy. Knowledge Management practitioners who focus on knowledge as a resource are especially concerned with how explicit knowledge can be effectively documented and managed in the form of data and information. They are also interested in how to best enable access to this resource for use and the generation of new tacit or explicit knowledge.

There is a vast array of technology available to support this Content Management, and we touch on this later in this chapter and also explore it more widely in the book as a whole. There are also rules or working practices that enable more effective management of the content. These rules include such things as version control, meta-data, thesauri and taxonomies in general. They ensure that the system functions consistently and that users can retrieve data and information in a comprehensive and timely way, but one that should not be too onerous. As we have already mentioned, this is likely to mean additional resource. But as this area is at the centre of the Knowledge Cycle, neglecting it will generate user frustration and ultimately a breakdown in knowledge flow. Again we cover these working practices in more depth later in the book.

Some roles that ensure effective Content Management include:

- Administrator or Curator – these are the people who look after the Content Management system: structure, access, the lifecycle of documents and so on. They may be formal data, document or information managers, or it may be an add-on to their day-to-day job.

- Subject Matter Expert – these usually work in tandem with the Administrator, and may even be the same person. They ensure that the content is current, relevant and useful to the business.

- Trainer and Mentor – the extent to which this role is needed depends on how intuitive the system is, and the general level of literacy of those using it. The Trainer gets people to a common level of understanding and performance. The Mentor provides additional support to those who need it. Sometimes local 'super-users' or champions who are experts in the system play these roles.

In our first scenario in Chapter 4 we describe the use of systems and associated processes to manage and facilitate access to the vast amounts of data, information and documents generated during Pharmaceutical R&D – and so to existing and potential new knowledge.

Such infrastructures will only work if people adopt and use them consistently throughout an organisation: if it is part of their behaviour, and of the organisation's culture. As soon as there is a gap, and an anticipated item of information cannot be found, then the system starts to be thrown into doubt and disrepute and people's commitment will start to wane. So there needs to be incentives: positive reinforcements or negative consequences.

Frank van Amsterdam's work has focused on people's desire to find information to support their work. He rightly argues that if people want to be able to find information, they in turn must ensure that others can easily find their own information. However, in any organisation, there is also likely to be a counter-force at work: where people are looking to protect confidential information. Thus effective policies, systems and processes are needed to reassure people, to make the associated work as easy as possible, and to generally ensure that the right information will be available to the right people at the right time. He says:

> *Nothing is for free: if you want your information to be found by others, then you have to make it findable. That is a cultural thing. It only works*

because people want everything to be found. If you don't want to be found, then no one will find you!

People

The importance of people as the source of expertise and new knowledge within organisations was recognised even before the advent of Knowledge Management as we know it. Rosabeth Moss-Kanter wrote about the 'renewed recognition of the importance of people, and of the talents and contributions of individuals, to a company's success' (Moss-Kanter 1983). She talked about the importance of people as entrepreneurs within the organisation both for incremental improvement and for innovation; themes that continue to be at the forefront today of organisational programmes of Lean and Six Sigma, business improvement and innovation.

The concept of 'Intellectual Capital' came to the fore in the 1990s through the work of Karl-Erik Sveiby, and through Skandia AFS's Skandia Navigator for publicly reporting its performance against measures for 'intangibles'. Melissie Clemmons Rumizen, in her book *The Complete Idiot's Guide to Knowledge Management* (Clemmons Rumizen 2002), gives a useful overview of both. The scope of Sveiby's work is substantial – one aspect is his 'intangible assets monitor' for measuring intellectual assets. His monitor defines three categories:

- Human competence – people's capacity to generate value and profit for the organisation as a result of their personal values, experience, social skills and educational background. Human competence is something that no organisation can own. People take it with them if and when they leave.

- External structure – the organisation's brand names, trademarks, image and its interactions with its customers and suppliers: how it is regarded externally.

- Internal structure – the databases, processes, models, documentation and Intellectual Property (IP): what is left at work when people go home or leave. It is what does belong to the organisation.

Skandia's Navigator echoes some of Sveiby's approach. It measures both actual performance and the capacity for delivering value through a range of measures: financial, customer (quality of relationships), process (the use of technology to create value), renewal and development (preparation for the future) and human. This last category alone included (at the time that Clemmons wrote about it) 61 possible measures to do with the productivity of people, what they know, their values and commitment. Quite a challenge! The topic of Intellectual Capital and how to measure it is something that continues to be a challenge, and continues to evolve.

Peter Drucker is another key name in the field of Knowledge Management and the role of people. He wrote about the concept of people doing 'knowledge work' in his book *Landmarks of Tomorrow* published in 1957, a theme that was subsequently picked up by others, including Thomas Davenport in his 2005 book *Thinking for a Living: How to Get Better Performance and Results from Knowledge Workers*. Knowledge workers are essentially those who earn their living through their minds: they carry out research, analyse, write, advise and generally apply their knowledge and experience to generate new knowledge and insights. They are continuously learning and helping others to do the same.

Knowledge workers are at the core of today's organisations, institutions and businesses. They are the intrapreneurs (internal entrepreneurs) that it is management's challenge to engage and empower so that organisations can continuously improve and innovate and so succeed in our increasingly competitive world.

Going back to Sveiby's definition of human competence, and their knowledge being something that people take with them when they leave: he highlights the importance of 'harvesting' this knowledge during people's time within an organisation, and of finding ways to 'retain' it before they leave. It is a common misconception that exit interviews can address the latter, as this is too little too late. The extraction of knowledge needs to start some months before a person leaves. A technique we call 'Ask the Expert' is a very simple and effective way to harvest and share knowledge between individuals who have expertise on a particular subject, and others who are interested to learn about it. It is essentially a structured approach, conducted face-to-face or virtually, where those wanting to learn about the subject take it in turns to ask open questions of the expert (who, why, what, where, when, how-style questions). People have found that they can cover a lot of ground in a relatively short time, and the expert does not have the burden of preparing something in advance but instead can respond to exactly what people want to know. Sometimes the expert is even pleasantly surprised by the extent of their knowledge! Observation, shadowing, storytelling and the availability of videos to demonstrate how things are done are other powerful ways to harvest and share knowledge between individuals.

A final tool to mention in this section is the use of 'yellow pages' or online directories of people within an organisation with varying degrees of information about their areas of expertise and interest. British Petroleum (BP) were possibly the first to introduce such a system at the time of their merger with Amoco to connect the thousands of employees across their global organisation who did not know each other. Nowadays functionality such as MySite in Sharepoint provide this and, at their most effective, these Expertise Location Systems enable people to connect to those with subject matter knowledge that may be useful to them. However, as with most Knowledge Management tools, they require support and encouragement to achieve the quality of content and active use of the system that will make them an integral part of the organisation's way of working.

Effective KM strategies put people at their core, not only because they are the stakeholders whose mindsets and behaviours need to be influenced for the change programme to succeed, but because they are the creators and users of the knowledge itself!

Having got the 'scaffolding' in place for our framework – the mental models, alignment with business strategy and KPIs– and also addressed the sources of knowledge – Content Management and people – the remaining two components are the building blocks that will make the knowledge flow. These are covered next.

Knowledge Management Capability

Any business function within an organisation requires resources to make it happen, and Knowledge Management is no different. In large organisations this is typically enacted through some form of central group, working with individuals in departments across the organisation. As KM programmes become more mature, the KM role of the individuals in the local departments may become more formal and, in time, the central role may become more decentralised, or absorbed into some other initiative or strategy for which this central group is responsible – for instance business process improvement, Change Management, innovation and so on.

Any central group needs to be sufficiently resourced to gain traction across the organisation and to become the effective process owner for Knowledge Management. There is no rule as to its size as it will depend on its remit and the nature of the organisation, and data on what others have done is very rare. Nick Milton of Knoco carried out a survey on LinkedIn (Milton 2011) on the size of central KM teams, and collected 41 datapoints. He concluded that there were two linear relationships. The first was one KM team member per 5,000 staff: this seemed to correlate to teams that were focused on managing the change and on introducing the elements of KM into the business, with staff in the business actively involved. The other was of one KM team member per 500 staff where the KM team also carried out a wide range of support activities, for example, Content Management. The KM teams play the Knowledge Manager role, rather than supporting the Knowledge Managers in the business, and in addition may contain web developers, e-learning specialists, and others who create, format or package content. At GSK Manufacturing we neatly fitted into the first category with a core KM group of five staff working with members of staff assigned with responsibility for KM at each of the 80 Manufacturing sites, covering the 30,000 employees involved.

The members of a central group and/or those with designated responsibility for KM will have the following attributes:

- experienced in the organisation;

- skilled in the tools, processes and technologies used to drive and support the Knowledge Management strategy;

- a good network across their part of the organisation;

- are good communicators and facilitators.

Above all they must have a passion for Knowledge Management.

Knowledge Management Tools, Processes and Technology

This section describes a number of specific tools, processes and technology to enable the flow of knowledge in the context of our two mental models: the Knowledge Cycle and Learn Before, Learn During and Learn After. We break these down into four areas:

- Learning Interventions that are usually associated with Learn Before, Learn During and Learn After;

- Good/Best Practice and Knowledge Transfer;

- CoPs;

- Technology.

LEARNING INTERVENTIONS – USING THE APPROACH OF LEARN BEFORE, LEARN DURING AND LEARN AFTER

As well as being a mental model, there are a range of processes and tools to support the different stages of this approach. It is important to recognise that the stages are interdependent. To oversimplify: it is not possible to Learn Before if there are no lessons available from Learn After!

RESEARCH AND BENCHMARKING

The key to the success of Learn Before is a culture where seeking out information and knowledge before starting something new is accepted and even expected. This begins with the expectations set by line managers and project sponsors that their direct reports, project leaders or managers will seek out knowledge, insights and advice on how best to go about the work, and spend a little time to save more time, reduce the risk of mistakes and produce a better end result. Managers are crucial as role models and can influence this behaviour by asking such questions as 'What useful knowledge or experience have you obtained on the subject?', 'Whom have you gone to for advice?' and 'What insights have you gained to optimise your approach?' The response to this may be 'What do I do?', or 'How do I go about finding useful knowledge?'

A potential solution, on a corporate scale, is to couple KM with a benchmarking programme to identify the location of high performance, and thus where to go to for knowledge and expertise. A simple and pragmatic approach is to generate a checklist of potential sources. Underpinning any approach to Learn Before is getting people to *ask questions*!

PEER ASSIST

A specific technique for Learn Before is Peer Assist which originated in BP and is particularly useful at the start of major projects. It is a workshop-based approach and brings together those who have appropriate knowledge with the members of the project team. The invited peer may have carried out a similar project or may in fact be removed from the subject area so that they bring a more objective 'helicopter view' and/or ask the 'daft questions'. The approach is well described in *Learning to Fly* (Collison and Parcell 2004).

VISITS

Visits can be used for Learn Before and Learn During. Their value, either internally within a large company or externally, cannot be underestimated. Getting an insight into other relevant operations can provide a range of ideas and be a great catalyst for change and improvement. The output is often a visit report or equivalent but it is important to ensure that the initiating organisation gets full value from the visit. This can be achieved by:

- identifying the learnings from the visit, that is, what was seen and heard or the insights gained that could stimulate improvement;

- identifying the actions that should be taken as a result of the visit in order to render it of benefit;

- ensuring that the learnings and potential actions generate an appropriate level of dialogue. An example of a visit stimulating dialogue is given in the section on Technology later in this chapter.

AFTER ACTION REVIEWS (AARS)

AARs are used for Learn During and Learn After. They were pioneered by the US Army during the Vietnam War, and have been universally adopted as a Knowledge Management tool. A team can use it as a quick Learn During review (10–30 minutes) of an event or task that has just been completed. The team leader usually conducts these reviews in order to prevent mistakes or to improve the execution of similar future tasks. There are variants of the AAR process but the most commonly used set of questions are:

- What was supposed to happen?

- What actually happened

- What were the differences and why?

- What have we learned?

The key to the success of AARs is to:

- carry them out immediately after an event – as everything needs to be fresh in everyone's mind, and in case the team disperses. This requires appropriate time to be set aside;

- ensure that the climate is right – people will need to be open about what went wrong so the session should be clearly about learning and not blaming;

- keep to the process and to the time allocated – it is not a forensic analysis, there may not be time to cover every aspect – prioritise;

- be clear about what is to be done with the learnings – is there a next time around for the team, can others benefit directly, what might be potentially useful in the future?

Throughout the process the important thing is to create a focus on the positive aspect of learnings, rather than the negative aspect of what didn't go as it should.

LEARNING REVIEWS

These are also known as 'Retrospects' and are used for Learning After. They are more comprehensive and reflective than an AAR and are usually carried out at the end of a project. They can take between half a day to two days, dependent on the size of the project, and make use of an external facilitator to enable the team leader to more fully participate. As with AARs, it is critical that Learning Reviews are undertaken as soon as possible following the completion of the project, before memories fade and people become too absorbed in new undertakings. Incentives, such as an end of project celebration, are useful to get people to attend.

Formats will vary, but the process is quite similar to an AAR.

- What was the objective?

- What was achieved, and if different to the objective – why?

- What learnings were there?

- What were the root causes of any problems/issues?

- What was the lesson?

- What needs to be changed for the future, for example, processes?

- Who needs to know?

A prerequisite is a suitable facilitator who is not part of the team.

Again the right climate is important with everyone, regardless of level, being treated equally and with respect, as people need to be open and honest with each other and able to speak freely. There will be disagreement, but the format allows time for this to be explored, keeping an eye on the objective of identifying learnings for others, and not assigning blame or praise.

LEARNING HISTORY

This technique was developed by MIT's Center for Organisational Learning (Kleiner and Roth 1997) and is another form of Learn After. It is basically a written narrative of a major event in a company, for example, a corporate restructuring or a successful product launch. The document is significant in size and is structured, in the main, into two columns. The right hand column consists of descriptions of events as experienced by the people who took part in them, were affected by them, or observed them close up. The left hand column contains analysis and commentary by the report author(s) intended to provide reflection and learnings. The technique is applied for collecting learnings from major change. As the collection and analysis of the resultant material requires a significant amount of resource, the benefits of using this technique need to be clear.

An example of a pharmaceutical application was following the shutdown of a site during a programme of rationalisation of a network of manufacturing sites. The Learning History was used by other sites that were being closed, and in particular addressed the question of why the site's performance improved after the closure announcement.

LESSONS LEARNED

This is a generic term for the output from AARs, Learning Reviews and any other tool in which learnings about how things can be done better are generated.

It is relatively easy to set up and successfully conduct AARs, Learning Reviews and so on, but it is quite a different proposition to ensure that the learnings are utilised. Factors that have to be overcome include:

- identifying who might potentially benefit from the learnings (and would they see them as relevant?);

- recognising what lessons might be useful in the future;

- capturing lessons in a way that makes their potential use easy to identify;

- identifying if the context is specific or transferrable;

- ensuring that the lessons are written in an engaging way (for example in the form of stories, or with a video clip);

- providing supporting information;

- the provision of a repository (for example, SharePoint) for publication and storage and active management of the resultant information;

- a strong 'learn before' culture coupled with ease of retrieving the lessons to ensure that they are actually used.

Motivation to generate 'lessons learned' will quickly die if it becomes apparent that the lessons are just going into a 'black hole', or if expectations are raised that a repository will always have the answers to a 'Learn Before'. This is a common failing of Lessons Learned databases in organisations. The business scope and benefits need to be clear, expectations managed and supporting mindsets in place. Examples of these mindsets include viewing lessons learned as an inspiration for improvement, for example, 'How can we work better on the next problem to hit us?' and innovation, 'What will prevent the next problem occurring?'

GOOD/BEST PRACTICE AND KNOWLEDGE TRANSFER

The concept of 'Best Practice' has been around for a number of years, and the transfer of Best Practices has been an integral component of Knowledge Management for some time. The adoption of 'Best Practice replication' at Ford

(Kwiecien 2001) has become a standard reference in KM, although not without some criticism.

GOOD PRACTICE SHARING AND THE TERMINOLOGY DILEMMA

An illustration of one of the reasons for the criticism is demonstrated by GSK's approach to Best Practices following the GlaxoWellcome and SmithKline Beecham merger in 2001. Knowledge Management was a key component of the Operational Excellence (OE) programme in the manufacturing part of the merged organisation. The OE programme focused on the application of Lean and Six Sigma. With many sites producing the same dose forms, for example, tablets, capsules and injectables, the concept of establishing the Best Practice for a particular operation was an attractive one. However when it came to the use of the term Best Practice, two key issues arose:

- In the true spirit of continuous improvement, if a best way of doing something can be established then it should only be transitory until a better way is established. In fact, holding up a practice as a beacon to be better than the way everyone else was doing it invited it to be shot down, or at least treated cynically.

- Manufacturing sites operate in different market conditions and to different requirements. For example, the 50 sites involved in the manufacture of tablets represented a range of technical complexity, cost pressures, volume requirements and design. The direct transfer of practices in this scenario was often difficult, impossible or simply not applicable.

GSK's answer was to use the term 'Good Practice'. This was more flexible, reduced the fear of undue criticism (although endorsement by an independent expert was generally required), and encouraged sites to look at each other's Good Practices knowing that although they might not be directly applicable they might inspire ideas for process improvement. The outcome was the creation of an informal Good Practice repository, which when benefits resulting from transfer of these practices were tracked for a period of one year, these totalled £3.8 million. A formal Good Practice process was also developed for the submission, independent approval and documentation of practices on a database with associated metrics for the review and adoption of the practices.

GOOD PRACTICE TRANSFER

The case study also brings to the surface another issue, but also an opportunity. In the GSK Manufacturing organisation there were many sites producing the same dose forms, some producing the same product for different markets. A Good Practice is only valuable, and hence worthwhile defining, if there is an operation that can benefit from its adoption. However, this doesn't mean that we shouldn't share our improvements and innovations. There is a big difference between defining something as a Good Practice and expecting it to be adopted elsewhere, and making an improvement or innovation and sharing it with colleagues, for instance in a CoP. In these instances it can provide ideas and inspiration for improvement in a different context, and at the very least prompt people to recognise that they can't stand still!

KNOWLEDGE TRANSFER

Knowledge transfer processes pick up on our earlier description of tacit and explicit knowledge. There are some well-established techniques available in transferring knowledge between the 'source' and the 'receiver', several of which we have already described:

- tacit to tacit – Peer Assist – a Learn Before technique;

- tacit to explicit – Knowledge Harvesting, Knowledge Retention – which we mentioned in our section on the People component of our framework;

- explicit to tacit – e-learning and other document-based training techniques, and individual research;

- explicit to explicit – as in the Content Management component of our framework.

There are certain criteria that have to be satisfied for effective transfer of knowledge. If the 'receiver' is the initiator, or is pulling the knowledge, it has to be easy to locate and access, and easy to search. If the 'source' or 'giver' is initiating or pushing the knowledge, they have to be able to identify what the potential value of the knowledge will be to the 'receiver'. This potential value also needs to be clear to the 'receiver' of a 'knowledge packet', in amongst all the other data and information that they will be receiving.

Another key success factor for Knowledge Transfer is how the knowledge is to be transferred. This includes the context in which the knowledge will be transferred, the medium to be used (a combination of media may be most effective), the conditions in which the knowledge will be received, and the opportunity for dialogue. Table 2.1 illustrates typical methods of Knowledge Transfer. It describes the options available when the giver and receiver are available at the same time (either in the same place or online), and when there may be a time gap between the knowledge being captured and made available, and when it is accessed. The ultimate choice may also be a combination of methods rather than a single one:

Table 2.1   Means of Knowledge Transfer

Synchronous	Asynchronous
Conversation	E-mail
Interviews and Verbal Question & Answer Session	Documents
Telephone Conferences	Blogs
Meetings – Face-to-Face and Virtual	Online Forums
Presentations, for example in Meeting and	Videos and Presentations (online)
Storytelling	'Instant' Messaging
Webinars	Guided Experience (including Apprenticeships) or
Coaching and Mentoring	Experimentation
Work Shadowing	E-learning

The transfer of tacit information presents many challenges but it is usually the 'make or break' aspect of Knowledge Transfer (see, for example, the product Knowledge Transfer case study in Chapter 5). We described several key factors for the success of tacit as well as explicit Knowledge Transfer in the Learn Before, During and After techniques above. CoPs also use both tacit and explicit Knowledge Transfer.

Communities of Practice (CoPs)

Our approach to CoPs is strongly influenced by the work of Richard McDermott and Etienne Wenger. There are many definitions of CoPs; this is one that we use:

> *A Community of Practice (CoP) is a dispersed group of people with a common interest in a subject who have decided to work together to share what they know, learn from each other and work collaboratively to achieve common goals. Their involvement with each other is voluntary,*

although it may be driven by cascaded objectives, and they do not have the same management reporting line.

Although a little wordy, this definition reflects several key concepts and some of the critical success factors for CoPs.

CRITERIA FOR A COMMUNITY OF PRACTICE (COP)

Unless CoPs are formed under the right circumstances they will not be successful. As these are covered by the definition, we will expand on each component of the definition in order to provide a set of usable criteria.

'A dispersed group of people … they do not have the same management reporting line' is one where people are not co-located or part of the same team. Geographic separation creates barriers to communication (you can't have a chat over the coffee machine) so the role of a CoP is to bring people together and build the relationships that can help mitigate these barriers. If people from different locations are on the same team, as can often happen in the functional 'divisions' of a large organisation at a senior level, they will interact regularly. However, below this level people will be part of the same organisation but less connected with colleagues at other locations, who may have similar roles. If this is to provide governance through common procedures and processes it can lead to differences in application and interpretation. A good example of this is Quality in Pharma where the European Union Good Manufacturing Practice (EU GMP) Guide requires the Quality organisation to be independent from Production, and thus it will be organised as one function spread across different locations in a multi-site operation. Similar situations might exist in other functions, for example, Finance, Technical or HR, presenting opportunities for CoPs, and these are explored further in Chapter 6.

'A common interest in a subject' is fundamental to an effective CoP but something that people often miss. A clear idea of the community's scope or subject matter is critical as this is what will get people involved (usually because it is their role or part of it) and it will be what the community discusses and works on. Members will want to understand and buy into what is in and what is out of scope. (McDermott, Snyder and Wenger 2002) describe the scope as the 'domain' of the community and a mature community can become the owner of this 'territory'.

The phrases 'who have decided to work together' and 'their involvement with each other is voluntary' reflect the fact that, other than in the case of the leader or facilitator, being a part of a community is not an appointment or an assignment. People involve themselves because they recognise that they can get something out of it. However, it is not necessarily totally voluntary. An individual may be assigned to represent a department. There may also be expectations of involvement, even coercion from within the community, particularly in the case of expertise and experience. The individual might also not want to be left 'out of the loop'. In the end, people get involved in CoPs because they want to interact with the other members and the extent of their common knowledge, practice and expertise determine their level of influence on each other.

The exchange of knowledge is the primary function of the CoP as it brings together people who are not normally connected. This is reflected in our definition by the phrases: 'to share what they know, learn from each other and work collaboratively to achieve common goals' and 'it may be driven by cascaded objectives'. This has to work in two ways. The benefit of learning from the expertise and experience of others is obvious, but what is in it for the experts, the early adopters and those who have learnt their lessons the hard way? Motivators might include recognition from peers, and constructive feedback or new insights leading to further development, potential innovation and generally 'keeping ahead of the curve'.

'Work collaboratively to achieve common goals' is critical in the development of the community from its early stages, and also to sustain the support from senior management to ensure its continuation. CoPs need to demonstrate impact and not just participate in knowledge sharing for its own sake. The ultimate demonstration of maturity of a community is when senior managers look towards it as a resource for achieving the company's objectives: it is recognition that it is a trusted and productive component of the organisation.

Common goals can also mean common problems. Working together and sharing resource to resolve common issues will enable problems to be resolved that may be difficult for one individual or location to address on its own. Common solutions also mean maintaining alignment of practices. Even if the problem is not a common one, gaining ideas and input from other experts and practitioners will result in a better solution, or at the very least endorsement of a planned course of action.

There are two other roles of a CoP with regard to knowledge. The first is sustainability. CoPs can provide continuity through the natural change in people and structure in an organisation. We give an example of one such community in Chapter 5. The second role is that of innovation: bringing together people from different backgrounds, with different ideas, but with a common desire to share these ideas and be receptive to others, provides an excellent environment for this.

CRITICAL SUCCESS FACTORS

Establishing and sustaining a CoP involves a complex cocktail of skill, good management, application and the right environment. There are five critical factors that should enable a community to make a good start:

1. The 'domain' of the community is clear and independent of the organisation's structure. As described above this has the dual effect of identifying the right people to be involved (based on their background in the subject), and defining the scope of topics to be discussed. It also needs to serve a purpose that is not currently being fulfilled by the organisation.

2. There is a clear value proposition for members and the business. Without business support the community will not be resourced or prioritised, and without a value proposition members' contribution will be minimal and the community will die. The value of the CoP must be clearly established and will range from the achievement of business objectives (as described elsewhere in this chapter) to personal development.

3. A sponsor and a leader are identified and committed. The sponsor acts as the focal point for ensuring business alignment and support and must be in place before the CoP is initiated. A leader must be properly resourced (usually 25–100 per cent of a role dependent on the size of the community), will often act in both a leadership and facilitation role, will have the appropriate skills and energy, and will also have a passion for the topic.

4. The CoP integrates with existing business processes. It is crucial to the success of a community that members do not see the community as extra to their already full workload, but that they gain access to new knowledge to help them in their jobs. The CoP also needs to be seen to be integrated into the way of working of the organisation,

for example, some existing activities and lines of communication migrate to it.

5.   There is a focus on building relationships. As people are brought together from different parts of the organisation on a 'voluntary' basis, it is crucial that an environment of trust is created. An effective way to do this is to organise physical (rather than virtual) meetings, workshops and events. Ideally this should happen at least once a year, although many communities have found that this has become more and more difficult due to the economic climate and cost reduction programme . Although virtual working technology has improved and become more available in recent years, virtual working is not as effective as physical meetings for building relationships, thus this remains a challenge for the community leader.

One final thought with regard to CoPs is that they will have a natural lifecycle. A good analogy is to think of them as a business. They thrive and perform well as long as they provide shareholder and customer value. When they no longer do so, they either go bankrupt or go out of business. Sometimes businesses get restructured and reconstituted during the bankruptcy process to something new and improved. So if the CoP is failing to fulfil its purpose, then look to re-energise it; if the need is no longer there then let nature take its course.

Technology

It is no coincidence that Knowledge Management has taken off since the advent of personal computers, and subsequently, the internet. Faster exchange of data, information and knowledge, and infinitely richer content than when we were solely reliant on typewriters, the telephone and face-to-face contact, have paved the way for us to challenge how effectively we can use our collective knowledge.

There is a little bit of a 'doom loop' scenario with technology in organisations. As we have already discussed, we should be structuring our KM efforts around business objectives. This means having the right supporting technology. However, organisations either invest in technology for a business purpose (such as Finance, Sales, Customer Relations, Employee Resource Management, Records Management and so on) with no real consideration of what value it could bring from a Knowledge Management perspective, or they invest in it for a KM purpose but without considering the underlying processes and behaviours that are needed to support it. As a consequence a KM initiative is likely to have to use technology in a way that is not ideal. Creating an environment where Knowledge Management is a more integral part of the business's way of working will naturally help to mitigate this situation.

We have already mentioned the role of technology in supporting the Content Management element in our framework and, to a lesser extent, in facilitating people-to-people connections in expertise location and collaboration. Our case studies throughout this book will explore these applications further. Systems and functionality are ever changing and it is not the purpose of this book to appraise technology tools, but here is a simple list of the technology that we are aware of at this point in time that could be incorporated in a KM strategy:

- blogs

- collaborative workspaces

- Content Management systems

- Data Management systems

- decision support systems

- discussion forums

- Document Management systems

- e-mail

- Expertise Location Systems

- expert systems

- information management systems

- instant messaging

- intranets

- podcasting

- RSS

- voice over IP (Skype) and videoconferencing

- social media (Twitter, Yammer, LinkedIn, Facebook, Pinterest, Google + and so on)

- survey and data collection tools

- webmeetings and webinars

- wikis.

The Knowledge Transfer grid that we used earlier can also be a useful tool for identifying which technology to use, when and for what purpose.

We have included e-mail in our list of technology, and it, as well as several of the other tools mentioned, can be a serious cause of 'information overload'. Collaborative tools provide a significant alternative in that they create a buffer (in the form of a repository) between a document or information 'giver' and a 'receiver' or user. Thus the user can work more on a pull basis, and so reduce their sense of information overload. This is part of a culture change to create and share knowledge on the basis of demand, 'just in time', the actual requirements of the receiver, or to meet a specific business context (a competitive advantage or a crisis).

Another benefit that the use of collaborative tools has over e-mail is visibility. The cc: list on e-mails can either be over-used, leading to information overload as we have already described, or neglected so that key people are omitted. One of our interviewees gave the following example:

If you use e-mail you're only talking to the people you think are interested. People perceive collaborative tools as something extra to e-mail rather than replacing it, but I'd rather have all my conversations on Yammer so then it's open to everyone. There was a really nice situation where a senior manager visited another company, did a really nice blog on what he'd found, and the conversation afterwards was great. Another senior manager asked a question using Yammer, and I was then able to sit and watch a conversation between two VPs, who are senior people in the organisation. I just thought this was brilliant. What usually happens at the moment is that there might be an e-mail conversation between the two of them, they might have educated themselves, they might have shared some insights, but the rest of us wouldn't have had a clue [that this was going on]. I wasn't wanting to comment, but just to see their thinking, and to see 'where your senior managers heads are' was great.

Many of the tools that we have described support virtual working in organisations that are dispersed, or need or want their people to be able to work more flexibly from home. Further, whereas instant messaging tools, for example, are hardly needed within small to medium organisations where people are mostly co-located, they might be of benefit where these organisations are working in some form of collaboration with other organisations.

As a final thought, it is the job of the Knowledge Manager to ensure that the technology is supported by the processes, practices and behaviours that fulfil the goals of both the Knowledge Management strategy, and that of the business overall. We remember one senior executive always telling his staff he wanted to be able to access any knowledge about his function in three clicks. However he never promoted knowledge re-use or transfer, or supported the establishment of CoPs that could have collated, managed and utilised that knowledge.

Conclusion

In this chapter we have endeavoured to provide an introduction to, and an overview of, Knowledge Management in order to assist those who are new to KM and to set the context for the rest of the book. There is a wealth of material available on KM through publications, articles and online forums, so there are many aspects which have not been covered at all, for example social network analysis, and other aspects that have only been briefly covered. To bring together the many facets of KM we have developed our own KM Framework. This chapter has described the content – the more tangible aspects of KM which most people will recognise as key elements of any KM programme – and we have been very clear that the starting point is to derive a KM strategy from the organisation's goals and objectives. However these stand little chance of success without the strategies and activities that enable the people within the organisation to change to a different mindset and way of working. We describe these generic approaches and link them to Knowledge Management in the Pharmaceutical Industry in Chapter 7. The broader KM and Pharmaceutical Industry themes are the substance of the next four chapters.

Chapter 3
Realising Pharmaceutical Value

Introduction[1]

Over the years, a number of Knowledge Management principles, techniques and approaches have been applied in the unique environment of the Pharmaceutical Industry. We believe that Knowledge Management will continue to have a role in the industry in the twenty-first century. To understand the nature of this role, and how it has evolved and will continue to do so, we must first get some understanding of the Pharmaceutical Industry itself.

The Pharmaceutical Industry has been undergoing a major transformation since the heady days of 'Big Pharma' in the 1970s and 1980s. Patent expiry, the rise of generics, and the decline of the blockbuster drug have all changed the landscape over the last 10–15 years. For research-based pharmaceutical companies, with huge costs and long lead times to develop new products, it has become a major challenge to achieve the return on investment. At the same time, jobs are being shed in the western pharma 'homelands' and regulators and the public are more demanding than ever.

The boom of the Pharmaceutical Industry from the 1950s to the 1980s was driven largely by research-based companies coming up with blockbuster drugs, for example for lowering blood pressure, controlling blood sugar and getting rid of infections. The last of these drugs was Viagra, which was launched in 1998.

Through these years this blockbuster model was a simple one: pump enough money into R&D and hope that your scientists come up with something that will treat a huge proportion of the population, and generate large amounts of money to both cover the experimental losses involved and reward the shareholders.

---

1   Introduction developed from views expressed in 'The End of Drug Discovery?' an interview with Patrick Vallance, Head of Drug Discovery, GSK and Professor Paul Workman, Director of Institute for Cancer Research, BBC Radio 4, 22 May 2012.

However, the blockbuster model is very inefficient: there is a huge failure rate (usually referred to as 'attrition') in the proportion of molecules from the early stages of discovery making it through the later clinical trials. Some argue that pharmaceutical companies were benefiting from the easily discovered 'low hanging fruit' which are just no longer there and companies are recognising that they need to change the way they approach the whole process of R&D, with all the challenges and new demands on knowledge that this brings.

In fact, there is a recognition that the Pharmaceutical Industry needs to fill significant gaps in its knowledge both about human diseases in general, and about the mechanisms of action of drugs. An indication of this is how many diseases, such as breast cancer, are being broken into sub-sets of mechanisms or defined states, which will ultimately be treated by individual medicines, as opposed to twentieth century 'catch-all' approaches. (An example is the stratification of patients and the rise of a personalised medicine approach for therapeutics, diagnostics and devices which we talk about further below.)

In addition, the patents from the most lucrative drugs are now expiring, and new molecules are no longer coming through at the rate that they were. With the financial climate exacerbating the situation, experts are now referring to the 'valley of death'. In the words of Professor Paul Workman:

> This is the valley between basic research and innovation on the one hand, and patient benefit and commercial success on the other, with this chasm in between into which there is a lack of funding and a lot of failure.

Some of the ways in which the Pharmaceutical Industry is responding to these pressures in R&D is to reduce costs by shedding jobs and closing sites, reduce risk by focusing on less risky therapeutic areas (for example, by pulling out of areas like neuropsychiatric diseases), and rely on academia to address some of the most risky aspects of drug discovery.

The Manufacturing element was previously a lot simpler too with most products being sold in the common forms of tablets, capsules, creams and ointments, liquids and injectables. However, over the last 30 years, the advent of generics has affected Manufacturing in several ways:

- differentiation of appearance – resulting for example in novel tablet shapes and different or more complex packaging;

- line extensions – trying to get the consumer committed to a specific product variant that is not covered by the generics;

- novel delivery devices – that can be patented and thus not copied.

And finally, there has been a shift in the supply chain for pharmaceuticals. In the boom years of the Pharmaceutical Industry, apart from a significant representation in Japan, most of it was concentrated in Europe and North America. Over the last 20 years Manufacturing in Europe and North America has declined in the big pharmaceutical companies. There has been a major growth in generic manufacturing in these areas, but more importantly manufacturing has become more globally spread, combined with a huge development of manufacturing in India, and to a lesser extent in China. The desire for governments to see products produced locally and reduce imports (sometimes using prohibitive tariffs), and the diversification described above, have resulted in more facilities, producing smaller volumes, spread globally and resulting in complex supply chains.

The overall result is a significant shift in the approach to drug discovery, a wider range of products with smaller volumes coming to market, often with novel designs, raw materials and devices being sourced from multiple suppliers, and a more fragmented, collaborative, or 'Open Innovation' approach to the entire pharmaceutical value chain. This whole transition in the industry has implications for all aspects of Knowledge Management.

In this chapter we will focus on three main topics:

- the evolution of the pharmaceutical value chain;

- how the KM Framework that we described in Chapter 1 relates to the Pharmaceutical Industry;

- the impact that the changing pharmaceutical business model is having on Knowledge Management.

The Evolution of the Pharmaceutical Value Chain

The pharmaceutical value chain has traditionally started from the identification of a drug target and some basic research (or 'discovery'), involving the synthesis of various chemical structures combined with biological assays, to come up

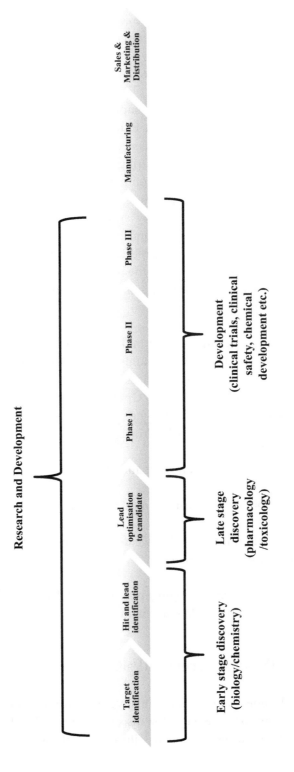

Figure 3.1 The traditional pharmaceutical value chain

with a number of potential drug candidates. These have then been sifted through further research and development to determine whether they have the desired activity and safety profiles, first *in vitro* and *in vivo* pharmacological and toxicology models, and then in a series of clinical studies to support submissions to Regulatory Authorities (such as the Medical Health Research Council (MHRC) in the UK, the European Medicines Agency (EMEA) in Europe and the Federal Drug Association (FDA) in the US). Further development has involved methods for scaling up chemical production and defining the best formulation, transitioning to large-scale manufacture, before final marketing initiatives to get the successful drug to the patient (Figure 3.1).

Whilst all of the processes used along this value chain have evolved in some way over the years, as we described in the introduction to this chapter, one of the most dramatic shifts has been in the starting point for new medicines.

FROM MEDICINAL CHEMISTRY TO BIOPHARMACEUTICALS

Biopharmaceuticals, also referred to as 'biologics', emerged in the early 1980s and 1990s as an alternative starting point to chemical synthesis for the development of new drugs. These biopharmaceuticals include proteins, nucleic acids and even living organisms such as bacteria or viruses. They are 'scaled up' into marketable products using biological processes or biotechnology.

Genentech developed the first approved biopharmaceutical, Humulin, manufactured and marketed by Eli Lilly, as a biosynthetic human insulin made using recombinant DNA technology. Other products include Abbott's Humira, based on an anti-TNF antibody, for rheumatoid arthritis, and Roche's Herceptin for the treatment of breast cancer.

One of the most advanced approaches to biopharmaceuticals is that of Kymab, founded in 2009, which is using Kymouse™, a transgenic mouse that has been designed to produce a diverse range of human antibodies as potential new drugs.

ALTERNATIVE IN VITRO AND IN VIVO MODELS

Biologists have traditionally used a range of *in vitro* assays to assess the potential efficacy and toxicity of new drug candidates. Primary cell lines derived from normal human tissues, as well as human stem cells, are being increasingly used to provide more informative data.

Indeed stem cells, with their ability to continuously renew themselves, and to develop into any of the cell types in the body, are an invaluable tool for not only evaluating potential new drugs, but for gaining a greater understanding of disease mechanisms. They are already used in bone marrow transplantation, but have the potential to treat a range of diseases.

Nor are things stopping there. For example, new advances in biotechnology by the Institute of Food Research and Plant Biosciences Limited, with funding from the Biotechnology and Biological Sciences Research Council (BBSRC) are leading to the development of a 'Dynamic Gastric Model' (BBSRC 2013): a computer-controlled, mechanical simulator of gastric digestion that processes real food, oral pharmaceutical and nutraceutical products (nutritional products with therapeutic benefits). This new *in vitro* tool will provide information on the interactions between the food we eat and liquids that we drink (such as alcohol) and the drugs that we take.

FROM SINGLE DRUG TARGETS TO STRATIFIED MEDICINES AND THE ROLE OF BIOMARKERS

There is a growing focus on stratified or personalised medicine: the concept that appropriate medicines, and doses, can be targeted to individuals, or as is more likely at this stage, sub-groups of the population based on their genetic profile.

For example, companies like Horizon Discovery have developed tools such as GENESIS™ to create human cell lines or 'patients-in-a-test-tube' that can be used to predict which patient sub-groups will respond to which drugs.

Professor Paul Workman of the Institute of Cancer Research comments:

> *The science is taking us in the opposite direction to blockbuster drugs, to personalised medicine. You would identify the patient who would benefit from what drug according to a gene test. A relatively small number of patients will benefit but they will benefit extremely well.*

Biomarkers are traceable substances that, when used in living cells or tissue, either in isolation or within a whole organism, can provide information on the effect of a drug, the state of a cell, tissue or organ, or the progression of a disease. Biomarkers can be synthetic compounds, natural proteins, genetic material or indeed any other kind of chemical or biochemical material.

According to Michel Goldman, Executive Director of the Innovative Medicines Initiative (IMI):

> *The key to pharma is personalised medicine with the development of biomarkers and the stratification of patients. To validate novel tools and convince regulators that a set of biomarkers might be useful to patients you need a very strong bioinformatics and KM approach. Also in eHealth, to manage the data coming from different sources, standards are needed: you need very skilled scientists in KM.*

CHANGES IN THE NATURE OF MANUFACTURE AND IN THE SUPPLY CHAIN FOR MANUFACTURING

The effect of the changes we have described for Manufacturing goes back to the Development phase where, as we describe further in Chapter 5, the shortening of development lead times and the need for a smooth transition into full-scale manufacture require increased collaboration and a greater flow of knowledge.

The other area in which there has been a significant shift is that of supply chain complexity. We have already mentioned the diversification of the product range in response to the challenge from generics, which results in a greater number of finished packs being marketed. This, combined with more sophisticated product delivery from Development, and more complicated sourcing due to the in-licensing of products, the out-sourcing of raw materials and the need for specialised components, all contribute to a highly complex path from raw material to finished goods. Meanwhile, there has been immense pressure on Manufacturing to reduce costs to compensate for falls in revenue from products going off patent and fewer new products to replace them. Amongst these changes there is also the need to maintain regulatory compliance throughout the supply chain, a constant challenge with the increased pace of change.

The Knowledge Management Framework in the Context of the Pharmaceutical Industry

Knowledge is generally considered as 'the other product' from the Pharmaceutical Industry. It is both the output and the input for the successive steps in the value chain. It has many facets, from providing comprehensive knowledge bases for the technicians, scientists, clinicians and various business services supporting the chain, through the sharing of advice and problem solving, to providing an environment for innovation and change.

A HISTORICAL PERSPECTIVE

According to a 2008 *PharmaManufacturing* editorial by Doug Bartholomew (Bartholomew 2008), most pharmaceutical companies are using technology and processes to capture and share knowledge in R&D and Manufacturing. Bartholomew suggests that a good Knowledge Management approach makes use of Document Management systems and collaborative tools to foster the sharing of ideas, experience and knowledge. The article cites AstraZeneca's International Biology Information System (IBIS) and Baxter International's Global Information Platform (GIP) as examples of the Knowledge Management systems used within the industry. It also cites SharePoint as an information-sharing platform to foster teamwork within the company, and its MySite feature to provide a Facebook-like online community.

Knowledge Management has also been an integral component of Bristol-Myers Squibb's way of working even before 2001 (Leavit n.d.), when Melinda Bickerstaff was appointed to lead a more formal approach to KM for R&D and the enterprise as a whole. 'Just no one labeled it that' as Bickerstaff quoted in an APQC article on the role of KM in new drug development. Their KM strategy combined the provision of integrated information products and services and training in their use, active knowledge capture and retention initiatives to coincide with the acquisition of DuPont Pharmaceuticals, creation of a lessons learned process, and development of a web-based portal for both published and internal information. The portal also acted as a vehicle for the creation of CoPs.

Bawden and Orna (2001) suggested that knowledge is required for three key objectives in a research-based pharmaceutical organisation:

- to identify new compounds for exploratory research;

- to determine which compounds have appropriate safety and efficacy;

- to bring the compounds to registration.

As the scope of this book extends beyond R&D, we would suggest an additional objective:

- to bring the new drug to the market, ensure regulatory compliance and maintain its competitive advantage.

Bawden and Orna see Knowledge Management as an extension of information management, dealing with 'knowing how', 'knowing who' and 'knowing why'. An adapted version of their list of the general areas of knowledge that are required in this context would include:

- Internal knowledge such as: a company's past and current research; its critical success factors for evaluating proposals and ongoing projects; developments in methods and technologies.

- External knowledge such as: regulatory requirements and legislation; the status of the health service and the Pharmaceutical Industry and its markets; customers; suppliers; developments in science, methods and technologies; competitors and their products; the social and economic environment.

OUR INTERVIEWEES' PERSPECTIVE

When we asked our interviewees about their experiences of and insights about Knowledge Management in the Pharmaceutical Industry, they tended to focus on two main types of knowledge: data and other forms of tangible or 'explicit' records (what we describe as 'content' in our framework), and people.

Whilst KM capability – or the roles played by individuals and functions within the organisation to promote and support Knowledge Management practices – did come up in our conversations with the interviewees, it perhaps has a less visible or centralised role in pharma today than it did back in the 1990s when it fell to IT, HR, Information Management or some other central Business Strategy department, maybe even a KM group, to drive it. This probably reflects a maturity in KM compared to 10–15 years ago, that is, that it is embedded to a large extent as a way of working; that the 'novelty factor' has worn off so that fewer organisations are paying attention to it; or that it has become more fragmented, more targeted. The answer may well be a combination of all three – with a challenging business environment and changing working practices such as increased flexible working, greater collaboration and more sophisticated technology, all contributing to this outcome. This is a theme that we come back to in Chapter 8.

Our interviewees also mentioned the importance and role of measurement frameworks and KPIs, and this something that we explore further in later chapters.

Last but not least, our KM Framework describes the importance of relating Knowledge Management strategies to the overall business goal. Whilst the case studies in the next few chapters of the book provide a lot more detail on how our KM Framework applies to the industry, we will give a more general illustration here, starting with business goals and Knowledge Management strategy.

THE PHARMACEUTICAL GOAL – OR VISION – AND KNOWLEDGE MANAGEMENT STRATEGY

Sandra Ward's experience with Knowledge Management started following the Glaxo Wellcome (GW) merger in 1996. One of the key goals of the new organisation was to build a Learning Organisation to realise the potential of 'our people, resources, technology, information and capital'. This goal and discussions with leaders of post-merger redesign projects in GW Research and Development stimulated the R&D Knowledge Network project that would deliver an enabling framework of work practices, processes, critical content, technical infrastructure, tools and competencies to support process redesign and business improvement initiatives. The enablers would accelerate the location of and connection with experts; the re-use of documented knowledge; reduce the risk of duplicative work; and foster idea creation and collaboration. The focus included:

- knowledge-sharing competences and techniques;

- location of resources – the top 100 R&D knowledge assets;

- standards to simplify information publication and location (meta-data, thesaurus, a single search engine, and publishing and alerting tools);

- training in collaborative working.

Benefits management underpinned all implementation streams to ensure that each delivered the planned business value.

(The terminology GW R&D used for the Knowledge Network illustrates the ongoing tension between the use of the terms 'information' and 'knowledge' and how many people inter-mix them.) In this example, the CEO's clear organisational goal enabled Sandra and her colleagues to pursue a Knowledge Management project, which in turn led to a number of related initiatives.

A review of a few pharmaceutical companies' current business goals, as presented on the internet, provides some interesting insights on where Knowledge Management strategies might sit today. Not all of them explicitly mention Knowledge Management, or even the word 'knowledge', but some of them do so quite graphically.

One of Pfizer's 'commitments for a healthier world' (Pfizer 2009) clearly emphasises the sharing of knowledge to address diseases:

> *Because answers to some of the most preventable health issues of our time are within reach, we will bring the best scientific minds together to challenge the most feared diseases of our time and as demonstration of this commitment, we will …*

- *Collaborate with others and share knowledge.*
- *Focus unparalleled scientific and financial resources on continued discovery, development, and, delivery of medicines that people need.*
- *Fight aggressively against Alzheimer's disease and cancer*

Merck's (Merck n.d.) value on diversity and teamwork emphasises knowledge as a core capability:

> *Our ability to excel depends on the integrity, knowledge, imagination, skill, diversity and teamwork of our employees*

Whilst the section of UCB's (UCB n.d.) vision that deals with 'Connecting People' (the other two sections focus on Connecting Science, and Connecting Patients) is perhaps the boldest acknowledgement of the value of the knowledge that comes from its people, and the importance of providing human and Information Technology-related opportunities to share it:

> *In a knowledge- and ideas-based industry like ours, human capital is the lifeblood of success. To unlock the creative potential of our global team of 9,000 staff and our partners, we are creating a networked, cross-functional organisation.*

- *multi-disciplinary teams are working on all development projects, including members of R&D, supply chain and sales, as well as partners and patients.*

- *UCB People, an innovative intranet tool, links our knowledge and skills. Our virtual R&D collaboration platform, based on the principles of Wikipedia, is another example.*

Even if they do not mention knowledge explicitly, the goal, or vision, of pharmaceutical companies today is all about knowledge sharing, and innovation and coaching plays a key role in supporting this.

KNOWLEDGE MANAGEMENT TOOLS, PROCESSES AND TECHNOLOGY

There are many 'touch-points' for knowledge along the value chain. In our KM Framework that we described in Chapter 1, we referred to 'Knowledge Transfer' as a type of KM process. We will use examples of Knowledge Transfer to describe a few of these 'touch-points' in the value chain as shown in Figure 3.2.

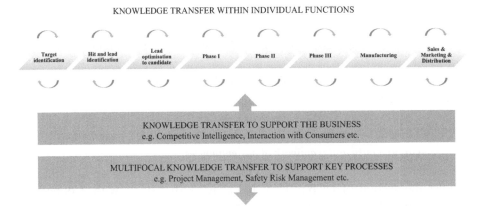

Figure 3.2   Knowledge inputs and outputs to the pharmaceutical value chain

Sequential Knowledge Transfer along the value chain

With knowledge being 'the other product' from the Pharmaceutical Industry, the ability to pass it along from one step in the value chain to the next is crucial. Some ways to achieve this are to have:

- project teams and 'stage gate' review meetings;

- well-structured Document Management systems for streamlined compilation of regulatory submissions;

- 'open access' policies so that people throughout the organisation have access to the information held within repositories.

As project team members can come from all parts of the organisation, projects are also an example of 'multifocal' Knowledge Transfer, that is, where knowledge can come from and go to any functional department in the organisation in order to support a common aim, rather than flowing sequentially from one point to the next. We talk more about the role of project teams in this approach below.

Document management systems facilitate the streamlined production of regulatory submissions, for example through pre-populated contents pages that 'drive' or 'pull' in the collection of the necessary constituent document. They also usually include pre-defined standards and templates that ensure that the format of documents is 'right first time'. The design of these systems reflects the experience and insights (the 'know-how') of those involved in what works best to meet the requirements of the Regulatory Authorities.

The actual degree of open access adopted by an organisation to the information held in its Document Management systems may be something that has to be negotiated in relation to any perceived regulatory or competitive risk. In Stephen Clulow's experience, the value of 'open access' is something that people recognised over time as they saw the resultant dramatic increase in the level of collaboration between departments, generally improved communication and smoother transition between the Research, Development and Manufacturing departments involved. He has witnessed savings of between two weeks and two months in the transition between research and development as a result of open access policies.

Effective Knowledge Transfer along the value chain is also integral to its efficient functioning. An example where John Riddell was involved in resolving issues with the transfer of manufacturing from one location to another is described in Chapter 5.

Multifocal Knowledge Transfer to support key processes in pharma

There are some processes within pharma which are either intrinsic to its way of working, as in the case of Project Management, or that deliver key information through the lifecycle of a drug, as in the case of Safety Risk Management. These are examples of 'multifocal' Knowledge Transfer in that the knowledge flows into and out of these activities from multiple parts of the organisational structure at the same time, rather than in a more sequential path along the value chain.

Project Management encompasses both technical Knowledge Management (scientific, clinical, manufacturing knowledge) and procedural Knowledge Management (the 'nuts and bolts' of managing a project in this environment). The most effective projects tap into what knowledge is already available when they start-up, access and share knowledge while they are in progress, and review what they have learnt for wider sharing when they are complete: essentially the 'Learn Before, Learn During, Learn After' that we describe in Chapter 1. This exchange of knowledge occurs between all the pharmaceutical departments represented on the project and their counterparts in organisations with which they are collaborating. We explore case studies of Knowledge Management in Project Management in Chapter 4.

According to Mark Perrott, Safety Risk Management is one of the big challenges for pharma over the next few years given the scope and reach of this for all the departments involved within organisations, and as the regulations continue to evolve. Mark wrote an internal paper based on his experience in this field that went into substantial depth on this subject. Some of the key implications for Knowledge Management are:

- the importance of proactively identifying, documenting and communicating risk information through every stage of R&D and through to post-approval, as opposed to the previous reactive approach for doing so only from the point of regulatory submissions;

- the need for an effective process which enables the consolidation of safety risks and related risk management actions and effective decision making at a senior level both within R&D and in the commercial functions;

- strong integration (information, documents, processes and general knowledge sharing) between all the team players involved in risk management be they clinical, pharmacovigilance, manufacturing or others.

Knowledge transfer within individual functions

Each function, discipline or step with the pharmaceutical value chain must find ways to manage its version of the Knowledge Cycle that we described in Chapter 1. A huge amount of internal and external (or published) data and information, expertise and insights needs to be managed and utilised to derive timely and well-informed new insights and decisions.

Accessing, making sense of, and managing clinical trial data are examples of some of the large Knowledge Management challenges faced by the Pharmaceutical Industry. Any initiative that can help trawl through the vast amounts of data involved and cut down on the consequent amount of time and money for trials is going to be very welcome. The IMI (IMI n.d.) is a joint European Union and European Federation of Pharmaceutical Industries and Associations (EFPIA) public–private initiative that has been set up to speed up the development of better and safer medicines for patients, by addressing these kinds of Knowledge Management challenges. Michel Goldman describes one such initiative by IMI:

> One example, which clearly illustrates the added value of public–private partnership for industry and for society is where the NEWMEDS project assembled the largest database ever on schizophrenic patients involved in clinical trials. There were more than 60 clinical trials, more than 20,000 patients and possibly nine different Pharmaceutical companies.
>
> What the project realized by doing a meta-analysis of the data was that a four-week observation, rather than the usual six-week observation, could be enough to predict the efficacy of the drug. They also realized that it was possible to reduce the number of patients in the trial. So this was a spectacular example showing that by working together, pooling data, organising Knowledge Management on a large scale it's possible to obtain very important data not only for organisations but also for patients.

Knowledge transfer to support the business

Some kinds of insights are needed across the whole of the value chain. Competitive Intelligence is a case in point. According to Tony Murabito, the ability to monitor what your competitors are doing, what they stopped doing and feed that into all aspects of a pharmaceutical organisation's work, has always lent itself to Knowledge Management techniques. He describes a 'technology' project at Cubist Pharmaceuticals that helped to connect the entire organisation by providing news stories, business reports and alerts on competitors, therapeutic areas of interest, and new research. The entire organisation was asked to provide trip reports from meetings, snippets from investigators and copies of posters that they had seen. According to Tony:

> *This is one way to engage and involve the entire organisation and share knowledge and information and give it back to them in a valuable format – which is the important part: how to make it valuable for everyone.*

However, the value of Knowledge Management is not limited to just within an organisation. Tony Murabito also describes an example at another company (Human Genome Sciences – HGS) of its application to the interface between a company and consumers in the case of Lupus, a very debilitating disease which manifests itself in fatigue, bone pain, terrible rashes, hair loss and at the latter more serious end stage renal cell failure and liver failure. It is very expensive and difficult to diagnose and there had been no new drugs approved by any regulatory agency in over 50 years prior to HGS's drug Benlysta™. So HGS investigated how it could bring experts, disease advocates and user communities together to share stories and approaches, and how to do that in the context of regulatory compliance and meeting the various regulations on communications between companies, practitioners and patients. Social media, still in its infancy but unbelievably powerful, is a tool for facilitating this kind of interaction between all the players. It is a new vehicle for communication and dialogue just starting to get some attention from the regulators. It is a subject we come back to in Chapter 8.

CONTENT, TECHNOLOGY AND PEOPLE

Given the vast amount of data generated internally by pharmaceutical companies (sometimes referred to as 'Big Data'), many Knowledge Management practitioners believe that the value they bring to the industry is in helping organisations to 'mine' the data, combine internal with external data (as in the work of the European Bioinformatics Institute (EBI)) and re-use it to answer important questions, enable decision making and facilitate collaboration within an increasingly fragmented market. We explore more examples in this area in later chapters, but here are a few to get us started.

We have already mentioned Document Management systems in this chapter, and record or Document Management is central to all organisations' management of their legacy in-house information as a potential source of new knowledge. The most basic application of Document Management is that every project and function has its own assigned online folder, with a common folder structure, especially at the top levels, to facilitate navigation by people who are working across multiple areas. Companies initially held this information on internal servers then migrated to Documentum, which, alongside SharePoint, continues to be a key technology for records management today.

Controlled vocabularies and standardisation facilitate retrieval of legacy information and hence the potential creation of new knowledge. Many organisations have sought to address this in-house over the years, but it is also an issue for sharing data and information across organisations, especially as the industry becomes increasingly fragmented.

Ann Martin has a Knowledge Management role across IMI, and so has an oversight of many of the projects that IMI supports. She witnessed the early development and eventual implementation of the Clinical Data Interchange Standards Consortium (CDISC) data format and content standards for clinical trials across the industry. It all started with the CEO of a small virtual company, Rebecca Kush, who, with the support of the FDA and a number of enthusiastic pharma professionals, started collaborating to define data content standards.[2] Now that the standards are in place, there is still a different degree of implementation from one company to another,[3] but the fact that all companies have adopted the standards to some extent has made a huge difference to their ability to share data[4] in a more streamlined way, and so extrapolate information and new knowledge from it.

---

2   The CDISC standards have been accepted for the obligatory data submissions as part of a marketing authorization application in the US (Center for Drug Evaluation Research (CDER) since 2004 and the Center for Biologicals Evaluation Research (CBER) since 2010. In the European Union, Patient Data Listings are part of the Clinical Study Report under section 16.2 and are proposed to be made available to the public under a controlled access. A draft guideline to this effect has been issued by EMEA on 24 June 2013 and refers to the CDISC in section 4.2 Data Standards.

3   Companies have implemented the standards as part of good business practice and for the purpose of regulatory submissions. Yet, as discussed in the CDER Common Data Standards Issues Document (version 1.1/December 2011), there have been varying degrees of implementation.

4   The use of standards does not only allow data to be shared with outside partners but also to streamline the analysis of the data and faster generation of the mandatory Summary of Clinical Safety and Summary of Clinical Efficacy in 2.7 Clinical Summary of a product registration dossier. The standard formats of the data and documents also allow faster assessment of molecules during in-licensing and out-licensing activities.

Intranets and associated search tools are very much at the core of so-called Knowledge Management technology tools today. An early experience of the successful application of intranets was to base the navigation and categorisation of information held within them on what people wanted to do, for example recruiting, accessing antibodies externally and so on rather than by organisational structure. At the same time, search tools evolved within the industry to Google-like interfaces, so that people could carry out simple searches with the option of doing more advanced ones.

We talk further about the use of social networking tools as a way of connecting people in Chapter 8 in particular, but here is an example of one of the earliest applications that we have come across, also described by Stephen Clulow:

> When scientists were part of a global organisation they did not know what everyone else was doing; the roles and responsibilities of certain groups; what knowledge, skills and capabilities they had; or what exciting and innovative science they were doing. So we used WIKI software to create a social networking site for scientists – this enabled everyone to share what they were doing, what they found interesting and it enabled them to collaborate (globally) to solve scientific challenges.

Tony Murabito builds on the theme of how to connect people in saying that the importance and relevance of Knowledge Management to pharma is in leveraging the technology in ways that were not possible even five years ago. HGS set up Town Hall meetings for Lupus, using newspaper supplements (*USA Today*, *Washington Post*, *Chicago Tribune* and others) and webcasts to highlight patients sharing their experiences, different therapeutic programmes they had been on, how they were dealing with the disease, side effects and getting back to living a semi-normal life, interacting with each other and with healthcare practitioners who were available to answer questions (managed in a way that was compliant with regulations). In Tony's view, these types of initiatives are going to become more and more critical as sources of knowledge to support scientific and medical advances.

KNOWLEDGE MANAGEMENT CAPABILITY

In the early days of introducing Knowledge Management as a strategic initiative within pharmaceutical organisations, which functional group took it on depended on how it was perceived: as technology (IT), information (Information Management or Libraries), learning (Human Resources), pure strategy (Business Strategy), or as a distinct entity to be managed by a centralised group (Knowledge Management, OE and so on).

According to Stephanie North, knowing where to place KM in the organisation can be a key problem in itself. Her experience is that it can often end up in the IT department because people associate knowledge with tools, rather than with the knowledge itself. However, as she points out, this can be a risk where organisations are cutting back, when aspects of IT can be the first to go, with activities relating to knowledge being outsourced, and the consequent loss of knowledge workers. As Stephanie goes on to say:

> *Pressure on IT to simplify, cutting back on the number of people involved (in IT and elsewhere in organisation) and focus on tools and applications rather than collaboration and the knowledge itself may also mitigate against the breadth and depth needed for effective KM.*

We mentioned earlier that the model for KM capability has been evolving in various ways, and one way that it has done so is to become integrated within other organisational disciplines – something that is generally a good thing from a business perspective. This situation can work well in smaller organisations where people will talk more to each other across disciplines and will also have multiple roles thereby fostering knowledge sharing. In larger organisations, it may result in the creation of knowledge silos.

However, a centrally placed KM group is also likely to struggle with sufficient reach across a large organisation. This can be mitigated by appointing and training local 'change agents' to promote and facilitate KM at a local level. We mentioned in Chapter 1 that a 'change agent' or 'Knowledge Manager' at each location supported the GSK Manufacturing Central Team. They were trained by the Central Team in the tools and processes and became an integral part of the strategy implementation. All bar a few carried out this role alongside other responsibilities, and although KM sometimes suffered from a lack of prioritisation by local management, on the whole the Knowledge Managers made a massive and critical contribution to the programme.

We look further at the role of the supporting capability for the KM strategy in Chapter 7, when we look at the enabling activities that are required for successful Knowledge Management.

Lastly, Stephanie North suggests that it may be worth considering the role of Alliance Managers in organisations in relation to KM because they have to manage relationships for collaboration with other organisations and oversee legal and other key data/information/knowledge exchanges involved in the implementation of these collaborations.

The Impact of the Changing Pharmaceutical Business Model on Knowledge Management

The evolution of the pharmaceutical business model has affected and will continue to affect the nature of the content and players in Knowledge Management. John Trigg suggests that it may be more than just a question of dealing with productivity issues, and that what the industry might experience may be in fact be 'game changing'.

> *There are potentially enormous opportunities with personalized medicine, moving away from the traditional 'blockbuster drug' model and targeting specific diseases and conditions, akin to 'The Long Tail' (Chris Anderson) – like the models adopted by Amazon and iTunes: stocking one of everything rather than large volumes of fewer items (a case of breaking the 80:20 rule).*

Quite how far-reaching these changes will be is something that we may only fully realise in retrospect, some years from now.

ECONOMIC AND BUSINESS CHALLENGES

As we mentioned in the introduction to this chapter, there are significant economic and business challenges for pharmaceutical companies. These include, but are not limited to, decreasing income due to patent expiry and a dwindling number of New Chemical Entities (NCEs).

The western world is also being affected by the shift in global economic centres to the BRIC countries (Brazil, Russia, India and China). To illustrate this, Cambridge Consultant's report from a recent workshop, 'India: Driving World Pharmaceuticals by 2030?' (Cambridge Consultants 2013), describes how India's Pharmaceutical Industry turnover has grown from $300 million in 1980 to more than $22 billion today and it is expected to continue to grow to $55 billion by 2020.

At the same time, as Sandra Ward says, there are huge pressures on R&D costs in companies as well as the changing shape of companies with more operational activities being outsourced and innovation being in-sourced, even in R&D. She mentions a December 2011 McKinsey report (Hunt, Manson and Morgan 2011) about the challenges being faced by 'Big Pharma':

> It uses terms like 'disaggregation of the value chain'. And that shows that there's a huge inherent knowledge challenge that you have to get right. If you're going to outsource, you have to be able to retain the expertise in-house to be able to manage that outsourcing. If you're going to in-source some of your new chemical entities, the process of assessment has got to fit into your R&D strategy. Essentially, these are knowledge-based activities.

Sandra Ward has direct experience of how Knowledge Management can come into play in out-licensing from working with one pharmaceutical company to help them engage partners. Conferences were the place where potential partners would reveal themselves through their R&D presentations, where knowledge of competitors could be deepened, and where corporate attendees needed to work as a team whilst scattering to pick up intelligence. The starting point was a consistent knowledge base of information on the compound that they wanted to out-licence. Armed with this the R&D staff could attend major conferences confident that they were up to date on all aspects of the compound. They exchanged daily updates with one another and with a home-based knowledge co-ordinator, charged with building up the knowledge gleaned on potential partners and competitors and ensuring that everyone could access it. This was used to help the company decide who their out-licence partner would be. As Sandra says:

> The whole in-licensing, out-licensing, working with partners has huge knowledge issues: sharing knowledge bases, securing knowledge bases, a form of managing Intellectual Capital wisely. Competitor intelligence is a key KM activity.

CHANGES IN STRATEGY AND ORGANISATIONAL STRUCTURE

Mergers and acquisitions, downsizing, moving to other geographical areas, outsourcing, the growth of biotechs and Contract Research Organisations (CROs) and collaborative models including 'Open Innovation' are further examples of the changes that the industry is undergoing.

In March 2013, AstraZeneca, Britain's second largest pharmaceutical company, announced that all of its research and development in the northwest of England will cease by 2016, with the loss or relocation of more than 2,000 jobs, effectively cutting more than a tenth of its UK workforce, and much of the relocation being to a new centre in Cambridge, UK. The US Company, Pfizer, did something similar not long before that, closing its science park in Sandwich, Kent, and shedding 1,500 jobs. GlaxoSmithKline, the UK's largest pharmaceutical company, has been working on its business model for about ten years, reorganising its R&D into smaller and smaller units, and again, shedding many jobs in the process.

Fragmentation and changes in organisational structure have huge implications for Knowledge Retention. As Stephen Clulow explains:

> *The KM roles that have been traditional drivers of Knowledge Management are those that tend to be viewed as peripheral and are being lost. There is less KM capability, and also greater pressures on time so that recording knowledge for posterity such as through exit interviews and After Action Reviews can suffer.*

At the same time, as Janette Thomas (an independent project manager who facilitates cross-organisational projects between small biotech start-ups, academia, health and pharmaceutical organisations) points out, there are lots of people coming out of pharmaceutical companies with the expertise and experience that enable them to fluidly come together and work as a team. However, as she also points out, this fragmentation poses greater challenges to those involved, having to work across different countries and cultures, and with every company having their own way of doing things.

This fragmentation of the industry, and the continued pressure on people from the efforts involved in streamlining the organisation and its processes, make it much harder to embed Knowledge Management practices. People cannot give the time and attention that are needed to facilitate and support the behavioural changes involved. We come back to this topic in Chapter 7.

Stephen Clulow also believes it is increasingly important to get Knowledge Transfer in place both in terms of what organisations already know and in how to manage the knowledge in partner relationships, with CROs, outsourcing, with collaborators and in joint ventures. He suggests that this Knowledge Transfer is also important because it will lead to innovation, something that the industry needs, not just to innovate its products but also its business models.

Finally, as Jackie Hunter says:

> *The effect of managing multiple collaborations in multiple companies creates challenges for KM. As companies work together more pre-competitively, understanding what is only within the company, what is only within a particular collaboration and what can be freely shared will be more and more important.*

THE EMERGENCE OF CROSS-ORGANISATION 'COMMUNITIES OF INTEREST'

In this more fragmented landscape, cross-organisation networking groups also have a valuable role to play in providing opportunities for their members to draw on and learn from expertise that would have been integral to larger organisations of which they might previously have been members. John Larkin is a partner at TPP, a small strategy and advisory firm. He set up the Biotech Speciality Pharma Forum (BSP) in 2006 as a cross-company networking group for people from IT functions. He says:

> *Although participation has changed over the years, the core group (Boston Biotechs) has stayed the same.*
>
> *The group is not trying to be a Gartner or other big research organisation. Such groups bring research to the table and are targeted mostly at CIOs with money attending one-off events.*
>
> *Instead, this group is aimed at smaller companies who lack the internal peer group usual to big companies. The theory they work on is that 'constructive peer pressure is a good thing'. Members therefore include relatively small companies (for example, Vertex, Sunovion, Cubist, Human Genome Sciences, Synageva) and are described as being from 'the office of the CIO' so that the CIO's direct reports can also participate.*

Janette Thomas has formed her own independent group of people to share information with – so it is her own management system in a way: a database of people. But more formally she is a member of the Pharmaceutical Information Project Management Group – PIPMG. It covers pharma and biotech project managers. They have meetings twice a year, have speakers and networking opportunities, and enable the sharing of common interests and Best Practices.

At the other end of the scale, One Nucleus (One Nucleus n.d.), based in the UK but including members from the US, other European countries, Australia and others amongst its network of 470 plus organisations, is one of the largest Life Sciences and healthcare companies networking groups. Its members range from the large global pharmaceutical companies to small biotech start-ups of less than ten people. Its regular events are valuable opportunities for its member organisations to hear about the latest developments in this sector and to explore opportunities to partner with each other.

Conclusion

The nature of the Pharmaceutical Industry value chain, and the entire model on which it is based, is evolving rapidly under the combined influence of scientific and technological breakthroughs, and economic and business pressures. Whether these changes will be purely evolutionary, or more fundamentally 'game changing', is something that only time will tell. In the meantime, Tony Murabito provides some useful closing thoughts:

> Health care is changing and it's going to be more about health prevention and how to keep people well instead of just curing them; what are the best practices, good nutrition, environmental issues and so on. Social media and Knowledge Management are going to lend themselves to that more and more. That's the only way we're going to get a handle on health care cost and be able to manage a growing and aging population.

PART II
Operational Knowledge Management

Chapter 4

Research and Development

Introduction

The R&D environment in the Pharmaceutical Industry is unique: one in 10,000 potential products make it to market, it takes at least ten years for them to get there, and a successful product can cost upwards of £500 million to develop.

In this environment, Knowledge Management can play a significant role in developing and sustaining product knowledge through the R&D process and into manufacture. It can also aid critical decision making and ensure that lessons are learnt. How does a culture of knowledge sharing relate to the individual scientist who is valued for his knowledge and expertise? In Chapter 3 we described how the model for R&D is changing with a trend away from traditional target-based projects, to a greater complexity in the nature of the data generated, and an increased collaboration across organisations. So how is the role of KM evolving in these new contexts? This chapter explores three scenarios that reflect the role of Knowledge Management in R&D.

The first scenario is the more traditional one that many people will recognise: how to manage the vast amounts of data, information and documents that arise during the course of R&D in such a way that people can not only find what they need, but potentially generate new knowledge as a result.

The second scenario explores ways to tap into the insights and experiences of the people involved in R&D projects and make them more widely available so that people can learn from each other and get more of a head start on subsequent projects.

The third scenario follows the experience of one individual in the changing models of collaboration across organisations.

First Scenario – Managing Data, Documents and Terminology to Facilitate the Generation of New Knowledge

Our first scenario describes how Knowledge Management-related techniques have helped people to access, connect and derive new knowledge from the vast volume of data and documents generated in the course of Drug Discovery and Development. In large organisations, hundreds and thousands of people are involved in generating, retrieving and generally managing this information. They work in many different project teams, over varying periods of time, and the volume of data and information generated is huge.

MANAGING AND ACCESSING INTERNAL DATA AND INFORMATION TO SUPPORT KNOWLEDGE GENERATION

Data, documents and associated information are increasingly generated and held in electronic form, bypassing what used to be the more conventional hard-copy format of laboratory notebooks and reports. This material resides in electronic notebooks, Microsoft Word and PowerPoint documents, pdfs, or in database and Document Management systems such as Oracle, Documentum and SharePoint.

John Trigg is somewhat of an authority on electronic laboratory notebooks (eLNBs). Although not originally from the Pharmaceutical Industry, John was working at Kodak when it became one of the first companies to adopt eLNBs. When John left Kodak in 2005 he came across similar experiences of the adoption and use of eLNBs in other sectors, such as the Life Sciences.

John's experience is that once you get the technology right, people start getting very enthusiastic about the new connections that they can make between the data, the people and new knowledge and, if you do get the technology right, it can start to influence behaviour. People find that they not only save time as a result of the technology and new behaviours but they also become more innovative:

> It creates more contact and interaction with others. People find that they are saving time and get quite excited by some of the stories and experiences generated. Though after six to 12 months, the stories start fading away because it becomes the new way of doing things.

The second thing that John has found is that the dynamic between chemists and analysts changes quite significantly when information is shared:

> Traditionally chemists have been quite defensive of criticisms from the analysts to whom they send their samples. However, once the analysts can see more information about how the chemists have generated their samples, they are able to provide more informative, detailed and higher quality feedback and suggestions for example on the possible causes of spurious peaks in the analysis. Similarly, chemists become less prescriptive about what they expect the analysts to do with their samples, and instead come to value and rely more on their expertise.

There are significant Data Management, records management and regulatory challenges with all of the materials associated with individual compounds. This is only increased by the fact that the data, documents and information come from all stages of R&D, both internal to the organisation, and from external sources. Whilst organisations have made huge strides in securing their data and information, the volume and complexity of this material just continues to grow. As a result, organisations are not only faced with the challenge of knowing what they have in their databases, but also with how to extract meaningful knowledge from this information. As Stephen Clulow observes:

> Companies are putting systems in place to mine written documents and document repositories for data, information and to look for trends as opposed to just mining databases. But the average scientist in a pharma company can't easily access tools to produce visual representations of the mined data or information. Visual representations are a great way to gain insights that facilitate decision making and to look for new opportunities.

> We are starting to be able to do this on a project-by-project basis: for example when drugs have shown safety but not efficacy in one indication companies are using data and text mining to reprofile the drug to identify different biological mechanisms or different indications where it could have efficacy. But, currently, it's very much on an ad hoc basis with systems that are hacked together just for that purpose. Greater availability of data and document mining tools combined with visualization tools (for all staff) would really help the industry innovate.

Some of the ways in which organisations tackle these challenges is through the development of controlled vocabularies, standard templates, drop-down lists for entering information, by limiting the amount of free text that people can use and by having tightly controlled processes for what can be entered into systems. References to diseases and therapeutic areas are particularly problematic in the range of terminology used to describe them. Likewise, the nomenclature used for compounds changes over time as their names evolve from the early days in Drug Discovery, through to the various names used once the drug is on the market. Frank van Amsterdam was responsible for a Dictionary Exchange (DEX) system, which provided a hub for sharing common values for vocabulary or terms across R&D within his organisation:

> *In large pharma companies people will use different terms for the same thing such as asthma/COPD without realising that they might be synonymous, and this will have an impact on searching/retrieval. DEX [Dictionary Exchange] addressed this for disease indications, pulling the terms from the MESH catalogue. Sometimes there might be as many as 20 synonyms – and the preferred terms will be listed in the vocabulary. People submitted new terms or values, which were sent to the curation teams for review with subject matter experts (SMEs) before acceptance. The result of this level of control in the records of data and documents was the increased success rate for the retrieval of information: people found a lot more information and had a greater sense of completeness.*

Effective version control and accessibility of key reference documents such as protocols is especially important in records management to enable the interpretation of data on specific compounds. The Good Laboratory, Good Clinical and Good Manufacturing Practices (GLP, GCP, GMP) that Pharmaceutical R&D is subject to also include specifications for the effective management of records. (For more about GXP and records management in the Pharmaceutical Industry in general, see Elisabeth Goodman's publication on records management as an information management discipline (Goodman 1994)).

However, managing internal data and information to facilitate access for new knowledge creation is not just down to content. John Davies explains how connecting data to the people who originally generated them is what really delivers value:

> *Examples of Knowledge Management at its most successful include straightforward ways of accessing other people's work. For example,*

scanning notebooks so that the compound registry has associated information from the notebooks (including the owner's name), so that this combines a formalised information system with creating the conditions for people to connect with each other.

The Pharmaceutical Industry used to be one in which people stayed within the same organisation for ten, 20 or 30 years, so that being able to locate people within the company to discuss related work was feasible even if it was not always facilitated in the way that John describes. However, with the greater levels of turnover and greater fragmentation that the industry is currently experiencing, these opportunities for internal follow-up will become less possible.

COMBINING INTERNAL DATA AND INFORMATION WITH EXTERNAL PUBLISHED INFORMATION

Organisations not only need access to their own internal data, they also need access to external published information. For Lee Harland, Knowledge Management is about turning the vast amount of data and text available to an organisation (the 'electronic substrate') into something useful or actionable. Lee and his team demonstrated how this could be done at Pfizer (Campbell et al. 2010) around Competitor Intelligence and Portfolio Management. They focused on the following points:

- I'm interested in this target.

- Which pathways is this target in?

- What do we know from the compounds that have gone before?

- Why did they fail, or what happened to them?

- What are other people doing in this space?

Lee and his team showed how data and information could be pulled from multiple sources to produce a chart that showed all the work going on in different organisations, for particular targets and drugs in different therapeutic areas. This opened up opportunities that people would not otherwise have had for out-licensing and in-licensing discussions with biotechnology and other companies. Many concrete projects emerged out of these discussions that might not have been otherwise identified.

SHARING DATA AND INFORMATION ACROSS ORGANISATIONS

The challenge is also to have some form of common shared vocabulary *between* the organisations increasingly involved in sharing their data. Ann Martin supervises the Knowledge Management projects for IMI[1] and implements associated strategies, which include the now reasonably well-established CDISC[2] data content formats for clinical trial data:

> *Pharma is moving from an enterprise R&D model to a networked R&D model. Moreover in terms of in-licensing, out-licensing, mergers, it is key to have good documentation of the digital assets at a minimum and ideally in a standard format to avoid having to convert the digital assets to a common format. I have seen examples of reusing legacy data that successfully answered questions in terms of redefining the design of studies, answering safety questions.*

However, there are other areas of R&D which still seriously lack some form of common standard to facilitate cross-organisation collaboration. Lee Harland's work here has been around influencing the vocabulary for drug discovery.

Lee cites a reference from Genentech (Sorani et al. 2010), which he says is 'massively illustrative' of where the industry is going. The scientists concerned sent some clinical samples to four or five CROs for specialised analysis, for example, the expression of cytokines. The role of the scientists was to marshal the sending of the samples, collate the data that came back and draw conclusions – so the scientists had a Knowledge Management role around these commodities, rather than their previous role of doing the analysis themselves. But they also had to manually correct the field data within several individual excel spreadsheets so that the data from the different CROs could be connected (for example, sex might be labelled as 'female' on one spreadsheet and 'f' on another, or different names might be used for a compound and so on). This manual correction was the bottleneck and it represented a serious misuse of these highly trained scientists' time, especially given that they had paid a lot of money to the CROs to do the work in the first place.

---

1 http://www.imi.europa.eu/content/ongoing-projects (accessed 13 June 2012). The defined KM projects at the time of the interview with Ann Martin were eTOX, ddmore, Open PHACTS and EHR4CR. Additional KM projects have since been added.

2 www.cdisc.org. The goal of CDISC is to provide open and free standards mainly for the use of collecting and processing clinical research data. The standard formats of the data and documents also allow faster assessment of molecules during in-licensing and out-licensing activities.

According to Lee, this difficulty of being able to compare data in non-standard form at the research level will only get worse. There are a lot of possibilities available to potentially address it, but a lack of will power to change (Harland et al. 2011). It is quite different from the situation with CDISC that we described above.

> There are many initiatives to produce standards for research but they are costly, long term processes and so it is not always easy to raise the necessary resources or funding. The returns are very long term and not immediate. The problem that this is trying to address is chronic but not acute and so it is difficult for management to see why this would be a worthwhile investment. But there are a lot of people working on this, in the field, it's just not moving forward as fast as it could.

This area has evolved naturally into another IMI project – Open PHACTS, which has just over 16 million euros in funding, and about 20 participants from industry, academia and small and medium sized enterprises (SMEs). The project team is looking at standards, how companies can work together and how work can be repeated. Addressing vocabularies is part of this. Whereas every company is using two to four full-time equivalents (FTEs) to download public data, standardise the vocabulary and maintain associated databases, Open PHACTS aims to do this just once – defining the rules for it, doing it properly and doing it in the public domain – thereby freeing up the FTEs used by organisations to do something more 'value added'.

This approach to standardising data at the research level will also help the smaller companies who are providing data and information products to industry. It will give them rules that they can understand and adhere to. The whole area of chemical structure representation is just one case in point – accurate electronic representation of chemical structures is difficult to do and errors in electronic structures can cause problems in subsequent data analysis. The quality of chemistry on the web varies enormously thus it is difficult to know what to trust, so the IMI team is developing standards for how this should be done too.

EXTERNALLY PROVIDED KNOWLEDGE MANAGEMENT SOLUTIONS

Some companies specialise in providing IT-based solutions to the Pharmaceutical Industry. One such, Aureus Pharma, a French company, was described in a European Commission publication (e-business W@tch 2005). Aureus Pharma supports the drug discovery programmes of pharmaceutical companies by integrating chemical and biological data from multiple external literature and patent sources into a single unified information system. As with the internal systems that we have described, the company has controlled lists, thesauri and ontologies to ensure that data are entered in a standard way and can be easily retrieved. They have 500 automatic procedures to avoid possible inconsistencies and they have an automatic validation process to check for missing data, incoherent data and outliers.

The result is that Aureus is able to generate databases for specific target classes that are installed at their clients' (pharma and biotech companies) premises and regularly updated. The scientists within these companies can use these databases as starting points for generating new leads without the time and cost of maintaining these databases themselves.

Second Scenario – Increasing the Project Management Capability in R&D

Project teams could be described as the engine of R&D: they bring together the people with the range of disciplines required to come up with a new drug. Their goals articulate the new knowledge or innovation that is to be attained: the target drug, therapeutic area, indication, unmet need, patient population and so on within the context of a timeline and budget. In an ideal world, the project team not only generates new knowledge but is also highly skilled and active in extracting existing knowledge from within and outside the organisation.

Our second scenario, which, for reasons of confidentiality includes two examples which are quoted anonymously, describes the approaches being explored by pharmaceutical companies to foster Knowledge Management in the context of Project Management. As Janette Thomas, our first interviewee says:

> Maintaining learnings in an organisation: what's happened, so that you don't go through the same thing over and over again – that's the crux of what Knowledge Management should be about. Obviously there's also the detail, which is about filing and making sure documents are looked after so that they can be found again.

OUR FIRST EXAMPLE

When Janette Thomas was at GSK she did some project close outs. There were some key learnings and they resulted in some very useful documents. Although the potential use of software and the internal internet to capture learnings was being investigated at the time, those involved in the project mainly just shared the outputs with their senior teams.

The close outs helped people to retain the key learnings in their minds and to share them with others, instead of just moving on. A facilitated meeting with everyone together for half a day helped with this and was quite effective. Although there was no clear formal process there were lots of individual learnings and the team members also shared the learnings with their line managers.

The Project Management group also shared learnings amongst themselves, which is not something that Janette has seen happening much in companies since then.

OUR SECOND EXAMPLE

In our second example, the interviewee is currently working in a group that is responsible for promoting and achieving Project Management excellence, and for generally increasing the Project Management capability across R&D. Knowledge Management is not mentioned explicitly in any of their job descriptions, but 'Learning from Experience' is part of their remit: the key things that a project needs to know that are not necessarily written down.

The advantage of having a central group with this kind of role in R&D is that it can provide training, facilitation and guidance to project teams in adopting this way of working (an example of the KM capability of our framework in action):

> That's where we who sit centrally in R&D are trying to bring in the process, so that we can actually put people in touch who wouldn't know that they've been through a similar situation, to try and act as that central point to make those links, and to use the technical side of it, the searchable SharePoint repository that we've got which is gradually building up the lessons learned and so on, so that people can see things in it from teams that they might not know existed but still might be applicable to their work.

The important thing in introducing this new way of working, as with any other, is to focus on the new behaviours that people need to adopt so that they become second nature, part of the culture rather than a 'bolt on' that people will drop as soon as other priorities get in the way. How this organisation addressed that was by identifying a key 'learner' behavioural characteristic where people ask questions and are willing to share their knowledge with others. It is not about being a victim to the 'bad' things that have happened, but rather it is about learning from the experience and moving on: the 'Learning from Experience' approach.

Whereas representatives from individual functions on the drug project teams will focus on product-related knowledge, this central group's efforts are focused on technical knowledge, processes and behaviours, and on interaction with changing R&D governance bodies. An example the interviewee gave was where project leaders held a session to review interactions with a governance body. Three teams that had been to the board described what went well, what they would do differently next time and what they would advise other teams to consider. The governance body secretary went along and did the same from the governance group's point of view. The central group is now following-up with the people who attended to find out what they have learned and applied and what impact that has had: the benefits or successes. As our interviewee explains:

> We're trying to sell 'Learning from Experience' on its successes and we've got one example where some learnings have been transferred between oncology teams that influenced a decision not to pursue a monotherapy programme for their drug. I have some quotes from the project leader of the receiving team to say that 'it was great that they did that, because we used that. It led us to not go down that route and to focus the product elsewhere, and cemented our ideas that we were doing the right thing in doing something else'.

Adopting this way of working also relies a lot on 'word of mouth' about successes: one team telling another about the benefits of carrying out Learning Reviews, and this team then approaching the central group for support in facilitating a similar session. It is not something that is taken for granted as these next examples illustrate:

> I had a phone call this morning from someone in clinical who is very active in KM, and he said that he was thinking about doing something in clinical on a large scale, and it's all around changing people's behaviours, and we want to do a learning exercise of some sort. So it was really encouraging that he was asking for our help on that. It shows that people are seeing that this is expected of them. It's also word of

mouth where people who have been through Learning Reviews suggest it to their colleagues in our teams, that is, 'that worked great for us, why don't you try it'. So we end up doing a Learning Review with them as well. We were doing drug project team Learning Reviews and that had a knock-on effect with an IS Team looking at early clinical data pilots (bringing data together in one place), so we were asked to help them. So it's really encouraging when this happens as a recommendation is the best check.

In addition, this group is setting up CoPs for project managers across R&D as a result of the 'Learning from Experience' initiative and other work. These CoPs will meet virtually, discuss key Project Management topics, help each other build their skills and capability, and help solve problems. This will be facilitated through a SharePoint site.

OUR THIRD EXAMPLE

Our third interviewee has a lot of parallels with the previous one. Although the role of their group is perhaps not so explicitly described as to do with project excellence, they are responsible for leading the development of projects, from a 'commit to medicine development' milestone, through to the lifecycle management of the drug in commercialisation. Like the previous example, they promote and support Learning Reviews, which they describe as 'After Action Reviews' and have a CoP for leaders. Unlike the previous example, they also conduct 'Knowledge Cafés'.

The After Action Reviews are run after every milestone in the project, and use a standard template to ensure consistency in how the information is captured:

It covers what went well, what didn't go well, and what would we do differently next time. Some of us have been through the loop of launching products many times, but product development is continually changing with new platform technologies and the need to keep abreast of changing guidelines/requirements. There are lots of things happening out there, so it's important that we capture this knowledge and share it with the next person coming along with a similar project.

In fact when any new leaders come into the organisation, they are encouraged to revisit After Action Reviews and to talk to the leaders and the members of the teams who generated them, so as to bring that knowledge and experience to life as opposed to it just sitting in databases.

The Leadership CoP is held every two weeks. It is used for sharing Good Practice and for continuous improvement. The project teams also use a number of management tools in their work, and so they also share their experiences of using particular tools.

The Knowledge Cafés are interactive knowledge-sharing sessions in the style of the Knowledge Cafés developed by David Gurteen (Gurteen, Regional Gurteen Community Cafés n.d.) . They're an open forum run on a quarterly basis, and are driven by a member of the interviewee's team. They focus on a 'hot topic' or on a project where there are some especially valuable learnings to pass on. Their emphasis is on stimulating the energetic tacit exchange of knowledge.

Again, as with the second interviewee, the focus is on sharing knowledge about the business of Project Management, rather than the functionally-related knowledge of the project team members. But the participants recognise that what works for one project, will not necessarily work for another:

> We are driven by a defined process with milestones: the way in which we move through the milestones, the way in which we do our day-job, which is leading teams, is driven by guidelines, Good Practice, knowledge and tools. All the projects are different. We say to new people coming onto the team 'One size does not fit all', because every project has got such nuances, and therefore at 'project team start-up' we offer them a suite of tools, we offer them knowledge, and they have to take it in the context of that project, and that team, and that project team, geography, and that therapy area.

Third Scenario – The Evolution of Collaborative Working Across Organisations

Collaboration across organisations is nothing new, but the extent and complexity of it has been increasing in response to the challenges faced by the Pharmaceutical Industry. Our third scenario traces one individual's experience of different kinds of collaborative models: between a technology company and the Pharmaceutical Industry, between academia and pharma, and in one of the many bioincubator campuses emerging in the UK and elsewhere.

Martino Picardo's experience with Knowledge Management, and Knowledge Transfer especially, goes back to when he was working at Amersham International, where he became Science Director for the Cardiff site. He started off as a bench scientist working on the latest, hottest technology in high-throughput screening, which was a radioactive bead-based technology. His first role was to develop an assay around cholesterol ester transfer protein – that assay went on to sell £12 million pounds worth of kits for Amersham into the Pharmaceutical Industry.

They found that it was very hard for commercial sales staff to sell a product that was entirely novel and based on very complicated science, so Amersham used 'white coat' sales through R&D people. These scientists were building people-to-people Knowledge Management-style connections. Martino, as the developer of the assay or screen, began the process by talking to people in AstraZeneca and other companies to understand the problems they were having. He worked directly with them on the phone or in their labs sometimes to help them understand the value of the technology and how it worked.

> If that had been left at commercial level, it would never have worked. Therefore Amersham ended up with a group of about 40 people in its development lab, with me as Technology Transfer Manager, on the phone, or on the road, and they had major contracts with Pharma. These were called either technology access, or early access programmes, where Pharma would pay a fee, for example, £100,000 for early entrance, or if doing a million compound screens, something like a dollar a tube. For Amersham this was worth a lot of money.

Although he did not realise it at the time, it was Martino's first exposure to Open Innovation. By the end of the third or fourth year, customers (Big Pharmas) were asking for workshops. They were happy for these to be attended by other companies. They used the workshops to learn from each other and to share Best Practices around a technology platform – telling others, for example, how they would use a screen for a kinase:

> They would blank out the compound name on the IC50 curves, but they would tell people about the hydration, evaporation, stirring problems. So Amersham had a robust high-throughput screening technology and the bottleneck became liquid dispensing and liquid handling. The major pharma companies were telling the liquid handlers that they had to

solve that problem. The plate makers were being told what plates were needed. That knowledge-sharing platform led to lots of developments, with Amersham being perceived as a data broker as well.

These workshops led to the development and engagement of a whole community of organisations and individuals centred around the then named Society of Biomolecular Screening. This collaborative approach helped Amersham, pharma, the scientists themselves and the evolution of the whole area of high-throughput screening expertise.

Martino's second collaborative model was working with the Technology Transfer group at Manchester University. At the start, about ten years ago, it was, as Martino says, a question of 'throwing' IP and university opportunities 'over the wall', and hoping that someone would pick them up:

The wall might as well have been ten-feet tall because there was no connection. Things then moved on when Universities built on their Technology Transfer opportunities and decided to add value before throwing it over the wall. They created some infrastructure and resource to develop their ideas in a way that might be more attractive. They found this very expensive and very difficult to justify to the paymasters within the University who defined success as tangible return – whether direct engagement and Knowledge Transfer, or directly through a spin-out. At this point there were too many spin-outs.

The happy ending in 2011–2012 was that GSK and AstraZeneca put £5 million each into the Inflammation Research Centre based in the University of Manchester but within one of the incubator buildings. The University also put in £5 million. As Martino says:

It's Open Innovation in research, and they've agreed to share the outputs and outcomes for anything coming out of it. The model has worked so well that they are looking to do something similar in another therapeutic area, also in Manchester.

This Manchester model is now recognised as Best Practice, with early engagement and investment in research, a designated person involved from the respective pharma companies, and not just being dependent on the Technology Transfer group to make things happen.

Now, at the time of writing, Martino is CEO of the Stevenage Bioscience Catalyst (SBC), sited next-door to GlaxoSmithKline's R&D facility in Hertfordshire. Jointly funded by GSK, the Wellcome Trust, EEDA (East of England Development Agency), the Technology Strategy Board, and BIS (the Government Department of Business Innovation and Skills), SBC provides a home for small biotechs, life science companies and start-ups. It gives them access to the expertise, networks and scientific facilities traditionally associated with multinational pharmaceutical companies in an 'Open Innovation' environment that fosters collaboration between all those involved.

SBC is a variation on the many science parks that have emerged in the UK and elsewhere. As Martino says:

> Whether it makes a difference to UK biotech to build one of these facilities next to a Big Pharma or on a campus or in a hospital is something we won't find out for potentially 20 years. The starting point was Government, pharma, academia all saying that the current model does not work: there's not enough engagement between the triangle that is academia, pharma and biotech – we now call it a quadrangle, because it's those 3 plus investment, and I would always put the NHS right next to academia as well.

Conclusion

We have explored three scenarios for Knowledge Management in R&D: the first focusing on managing data and information to facilitate the generation of new knowledge, the second exploring the sharing of knowledge between those involved in project teams, and the third tracing the evolution of collaborative working and Knowledge Transfer across organisations.

The three scenarios between them illustrate many aspects of the knowledge framework that we described in Chapter 2: the role of 'content' and 'people' in relation to knowledge; the way processes, technology and people with a KM capability are instrumental in facilitating the transfer of knowledge; and how the KM strategies used support business goals and objectives. In addition, the examples we have used in these scenarios reflect the changing pharmaceutical environment that we introduced in Chapter 3. The next two chapters will continue to illustrate these themes with further examples taken from other areas of the Pharmaceutical Industry.

Chapter 5
Manufacturing

Introduction

As described in Chapter 1, it is critical to have tangible business objectives as the starting point for any KM activity, initiative or programme. However we would suggest that there are four generic main areas where KM can add value to pharmaceutical manufacturing:

- the management of product and process knowledge over the lifecycle of the product;

- product transfer;

- Communities of Practice (CoPs);

- Good (or Best) Practice Transfer.

We will now consider each of these except for Good Practice Transfer which is covered in Chapter 6.

Product and Process Knowledge Management

Historically, this is an area where there has been a huge degree of variation, both between companies, and between locations and products. Typically older, established products have a minimum of associated documentation, having been produced for a number of years on the same equipment, and with the knowledge and experience developed by operator and technical staff able to compensate for any issues or abnormalities. Newer products have traceable development work, but the complexity is usually higher and there is less experience of dealing with process variation and different conditions for manufacture, for example at different locations. All of this leads to a complex scenario for managing the knowledge that enables successful and consistent manufacture of products.

A very significant change in this area came about when revised EU GMP Guidelines came into force on 31 January 2013. These included the incorporation of International Conference on Harmonisation of Technical Requirements for Registration of Pharmaceuticals for Human Use (ICH) Tripartide Guideline Q10 – Product Quality System (PQS) (ICH Harmonised Tripartite Guideline 2008) into Chapter 1 of the guideline, which is now re-named Pharmaceutical Quality System (Eudralex Volume 4 2012)

The revised Guidelines contain the following:

> *A Pharmaceutical Quality System appropriate for the manufacture of medicinal products should ensure that ... Product and process knowledge is managed throughout all lifecycle stages ... Continual improvement is facilitated through the implementation of quality improvements appropriate to the current level of process and product knowledge.*

It also states

> *ICH Q10 is reproduced in Part III of the Guide and can be used to supplement the contents of this chapter.*

ICH Q10 specifies Knowledge Management (along with Quality Risk Management (ICH Q9)) as an enabler to the achievement of the three objectives of ICH Q10:

- achieve product realisation;

- establish and maintain a state of control;

- facilitate continual improvement.

It specifies the role of Knowledge Management as:

> *Facilitating achievement of the objectives by providing the means for science and risk-based decisions related to product quality.*

It also clearly states how Knowledge Management relates to product and process knowledge:

> *Product and process knowledge should be managed from development through the commercial life of the product up to and including product discontinuation. For example, development activities using scientific approaches provide knowledge for product and process understanding. Knowledge management is a systematic approach to acquiring, analysing, storing and disseminating information related to products, manufacturing processes and components. Sources of knowledge include, but are not limited to prior knowledge (public domain or internally documented); pharmaceutical development studies; Technology Transfer activities; process validation studies over the product lifecycle; manufacturing experience; innovation; continual improvement; and Change Management activities.*

This provides a clear mandate for a Knowledge Management system associated with product and process knowledge. As it references the product lifecycle and incorporates product development, it is useful also to refer to ICH Q8 (ICH Harmonised Tripartite Guideline 2009) which references Quality by Design and its links to Knowledge Management:

> *A more systematic approach to development (also defined as Quality by Design) can include, for example, incorporation of prior knowledge, results of studies using design of experiments, use of quality risk management, and use of Knowledge Management (see ICH Q10) throughout the lifecycle of the product. Such a systematic approach can enhance achieving the desired quality of the product and help the regulators to better understand a company's strategy. Product and process understanding can be updated with the knowledge gained over the product lifecycle.*

This systematic approach can include product design guidance so that dose forms are made in a standardised way that reflects existing knowledge of materials and formulation, that is, existing science, and experience with scale-up and realisation of manufacture on a commercial scale.

In linking the essential elements of ICH, they can be represented by the following diagram.

Figure 5.1   International   Conference   on   Harmonisation   and Knowledge Management

A Knowledge Management system for a Pharmaceutical Quality System should have the following attributes:

- **A responsible person** such as a Product Owner, who has clearly defined responsibilities with regard to maintaining product and process knowledge throughout its lifecycle

- **A Content Management system** with a clearly defined structure and taxonomy so that documents can be added and become integrated into a coherent system where retrieval of knowledge on a topic is straightforward.

- Plan for the **transitions in technology.** At some point your Document Management system will be replaced!

- **Clearly defined procedures** for identifying appropriate documents, adding and retrieving, together with processes for lifecycle maintenance, integrated into the GMP training system.

- **Periodic technical reviews** using assessment tools, for example, Britest, to identify knowledge gaps.

- Identification of the knowledge and expertise held by individuals, that is, **tacit knowledge,** and processes for capturing when they move on from responsibilities associated with the product/process.

A structured discussion at the Henley Knowledge Management Forum a few years ago developed some insights into managing explicit knowledge, particularly over the long term, which has relevance to the challenge of managing product knowledge through its lifecycle. A key output was 'half-life, not shelf-life', that is, the relevance of captured knowledge will diminish with time. There are regulations about the retention of records, but the thought here is that in maintaining working product and process knowledge we should focus on documents which have a significant value, rather than minimal value.

To put the maintenance of knowledge into context it is useful to contrast the business of pharmaceuticals as a long-term one, as opposed to companies like Oracle. Oracle, a computer software and hardware company, have estimated that only 10–15 per cent of their knowledge has a shelf-life greater than three months, whereas it is common practice for pharmaceutical companies to retain their production records for seven years, and R&D records may last 50 years. However, managing product and process knowledge over long periods is not unique to the Pharmaceutical Industry. There are other industries that have similar long lifecycles, for example, aerospace, nuclear, with which pharmaceuticals can benchmark, identify Good Practice and gain ideas.

The following case study illustrates a simple system to create Product and Process Knowledge Maps using standard desktop software, which was triggered by the transfer of a new product from R&D to Manufacturing. It provides a powerful but pragmatic example of Content Management that is a component of our KM Framework described in Chapter 1.

CASE STUDY – PRODUCT AND PROCESS KNOWLEDGE MAPS

The initiative, which was implemented in several pilots, was to map the process (usually to two/three levels of detail) using PowerPoint. A user could start at the top level and using hyperlinks work down through levels of detail represented in the process diagrams (all in block diagram form) to the desired element of the process. When this was reached a further hyperlink could be selected to go to a slide of the process parameters for that step. Further hyperlinks would go to the reports, documents, photographs and video clips that represented the knowledge of *why* that step is carried out as specified in the manufacturing instructions.

A set of templates was created in order to keep the knowledge maps standardised and PowerPoint-based training modules provided for easy uptake of the concept. The basic level principles of the five level structure are shown in Figure 5.2 below:

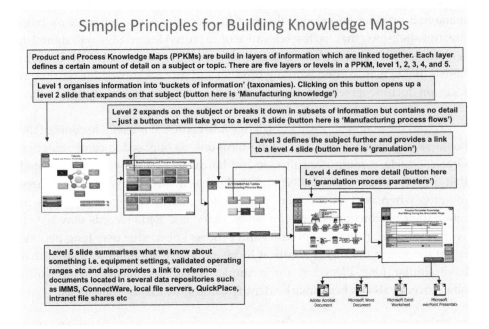

Figure 5.2   Simple principles for building Knowledge Maps

The advantages of this approach are:

- once a map has been created for a product in one dose form, the slides can be easily copied, adapted and re-used;

- it is visual;

- it is 'low-tech' and thus can be generated and utilised widely;

- due to the use of standard Microsoft software, issues with longevity and updating are likely to be minimal.

Although there was encouragement to add comments and ad-hoc information into the system, usage in the pilots was confined to mapping documents. There was a lot of enthusiasm for this approach amongst those who were involved with it. However, although an array of templates were designed, the population of the Knowledge Map for a product required a significant amount of resource, and at the time the groundwork was concluded the company was going through a significant cost and headcount reduction programme. As a consequence, the authors understand that the approach has not been used beyond the products on which it was piloted.

Product Transfer

Managing the product through its lifecycle may result in up to three types of critical Knowledge Transfer:

- R&D to Manufacturing (in the case of a research-based company);

- between Manufacturing locations (in the same company);

- between an 'owner' company and third-party manufacturer.

The third category, from a Knowledge Management perspective, will be very similar to the second. However the nature of the relationship (and contract!) between the companies will heavily influence the process. There will also be involvement of other functions, for example, Logistics and Procurement. For the purposes of this book we will consider the issues involved in Knowledge Transfer in the first two categories.

LINKING R&D AND MANUFACTURING

With the challenges facing the Pharmaceutical Industry, one of the key opportunity areas has been the transition of products from R&D to Manufacturing, both in terms of shortening timescales and increasing process robustness. This is always likely to be a difficult area between units of the business that operate with different drivers. As we have discussed in Chapter 4, the environment for product development has, and is continuing, to change significantly. Across the industry companies have taken measures to eliminate any 'throw it over the wall' mentality, and make improvements to the development, transfer and manufacturing start-up processes. This has a 'knock-on' effect with Manufacturing which has led to a change in involvement as Barry Hardy describes:

> *Transfer of technology between Development and Manufacturing is now a key success factor to achieve robust processes and minimise cost of goods. This demands standardisation of equipment, processes and materials between Development and Manufacturing, but also much greater interaction and dialogue from the earliest days of new product development. In the past this involved having experts from Manufacturing participate in Development project teams, often attending meetings during which their input was minimal and for projects for which the success likelihood was low. In manufacturing parlance this process is not fit for purpose and a better way of sharing and managing knowledge is needed. (Hardy 2005)*

The solution adopted by many companies is the implementation of concepts such as 'Design for Manufacture' (DFM) which have been in use for over 30 years in industries such as automotive and electronics. Most of the cost of a product is locked in early during the design phase. The application of DFM and other techniques recognises that consideration of manufacturing options and constraints at an early stage reduces the number of issues downstream where the opportunity to optimise production processes post-launch are minimal.

Strengthening the integration between Technical Development and Manufacturing operations will not just bring benefits in faster product throughput times, robust processes and better process control, all of which will reduce cost, but it is also expected by the regulators. Barry continues:

> *Knowledge Management is key to making this work. R&D functions need to have a better understanding of preferred standards in equipment and materials used by Technical Operations; on the other hand Technical Operations need adequate warning of new product technologies which might require new investments or the selection of strategic outsourcing partners. In the past the high attrition rates suffered by early phase compounds made it difficult to set priorities and allocate time for technical operations' involvement in development projects. This cannot be allowed to continue because development times are reducing with the implication that the launch molecule and formulation need to be finalised relatively early.*

Whilst the linkages Barry describes are now in place in many companies, many challenges remain, not least of which may be different Document Management systems. As already mentioned, the assignment of a Product Owner from Manufacturing whilst the product is in development can help the flow of knowledge. If R&D maintains responsibility for the process whilst it is in the early stages of manufacture, this can ensure that maximum value is extracted from the technical knowledge of the Development team.

SECONDARY TRANSFER OF PRODUCTS BETWEEN LOCATIONS WITHIN THE MANUFACTURING ORGANISATION

This is an area with a huge range of situations and complexity, however what is clear is the need for strategies for explicit and tacit knowledge.

At one extreme is the establishment of contract packing in Europe for bulk tablets supplied from Japan at Otsuka Pharmaceuticals where Steve Friend, Head of QA and Technical Operations, Europe has the following approach:

> For technical and product knowledge my key source is the CMC section within the marketing authorisation where all the important data that drives the regulatory agency resides, for example, description of the process, the manufacturing sites. Then if I have any specific questions I have regulatory, technical and quality colleagues in Japan I can go to for any further information.

In more complex situations it can be easy to focus on ensuring that the large volume of documentation is effectively transferred and lose sight of the importance of tacit knowledge, as illustrated by the following case study.

CASE STUDY – HOW KNOWLEDGE MANAGEMENT SOLVED ISSUES WITH PRODUCT TRANSFER

Following a large corporate merger, a huge rationalisation programme was undertaken in the manufacturing organisation which involved the closure of circa 50 sites. It not only resulted in the redistribution of product manufacture and packing from these sites, but also a realignment of activities between those remaining.

When product transfers were to occur the official process was that this should be site-to-site, however there was often significant facilitation by central groups (Technical and to a lesser extent Quality and Engineering). The relationships between the central groups were good and well established so information generally flowed, although it was also dependent upon the strength of the technical resource at the receiving site. The Technical group maintained a system of central process documentation which was used as both a reference point and added to with information from the transfers.

During the latter stages of the programme, when the transfer of manufacture of more complex products was at its peak and the resources supporting the transfers had been reduced, it began to emerge that the start up at the new location was not always producing consistently good product. An analysis of four transfers showed that the root cause of poor transfers related to two key steps – Technical Evaluation and Knowledge Transfer. Fundamentally, transfers were relying on documents and correspondence resulting in the transfer of tacit knowledge being neglected. There was also an insufficient building of process understanding to overcome the changes in operational plant and equipment.

The Knowledge Management Team was approached to input techniques and help design processes. They had already developed the Knowledge Market processes (primarily for use in CoPs – see Chapter 6) and these were adapted into the process for Product Knowledge Transfer. Using the principles of the Knowledge Cycle described in Chapter 1, emphasis was placed on surfacing and capturing the tacit knowledge of operators and technicians, and capturing knowledge into a repository that the receiving site could use for continuing to build its knowledge on the manufacture of the product. This approach proved very successful not only in identifying what was known about the manufacture of the product, but also what was not known.

A revised process was piloted in three transfers with a face-to-face Knowledge Transfer workshop at the donating site involving technical and operational staff. The workshop was designed around the construction of a Knowledge Map consisting of ten elements. These workshops lasted two to three days and included a visit to the donor site operations and discussion of the process detail with production operators.

The result was a 'blueprint' for all future transfers with processes for the surfacing and transfer of tacit knowledge at the heart of it. This blueprint has now become the standard process for product transfers.

Communities of Practice (CoPs)

CoPs are a key Knowledge Management tool and are well described in Chapter 1. Their importance in Manufacturing is heightened by:

- the attention in recent years paid by regulatory bodies to any differences in the Manufacturing process between locations for a particular product;

- the potential for the CoP to build relationships across the Operations, Technical and Quality functions to enable better solutions to be developed and to solve problems more quickly;

- the further opportunity they provide to link Development and Manufacturing.

We will now look at three CoPs that had different reasons for success in Manufacturing in GSK as examples of how CoPs can help a manufacturing organisation.

THE COMMUNITIES OF PRACTICE (COPS) THAT SURVIVED IN GSK (A CASE HISTORY OF THE AEROSOL MANUFACTURING EXCELLENCE FORUM)

This group started life in the early 1990s when the company formed a set of Technology Liaison Groups (TLGs) to link together sites manufacturing the same dose forms/products and the Development teams bringing new products out of R&D. Some foundered, or never really got going, but the Inhaled Products and Cephalosporin TLGs had a good degree of success.

The original objective of the TLGs was to pursue technical innovation and groups were set up by dose form. Although the groups were established, the pursuit of technical innovation was not achieved for a variety of reasons, and most groups gravitated towards a focus on sharing their current issues and continuous improvement initiatives. Where interest in new technology was established, the initiation of projects generally failed due to lack of financial support to even explore feasibility.

When one looks at what has happened to the different groups the themes identifying a 'common interest' and recognising the *need* to work with others emerges. In all of the groups participants agreed that coming together and sharing issues and solutions was valuable, but there was little true transfer from site-to-site of these solutions. Good ideas that were shared usually fell victim to resistance or the 'Not Invented Here' syndrome and were not implemented, or were implemented in different ways at different sites.

In the TLGs that failed there were a range of sites which produce on the whole different products on different equipment for different customer bases. At that time there was no manufacturing organisation, all the sites outside of the UK were a part of the local company. During the rapid expansion of Glaxo in the 1970s and 1980s, this model worked well as the sites were able to be closely coupled to the local commercial operation. However as the sites were all managed and funded independently, there was little incentive to co-operate with other sites to introduce common ways of working until the formation of a global manufacturing organisation in the late 1990s.

Up until this time the Inhaled Products TLG had been focused on finding common ground, establishing standard processes then disseminating these out to other operations. It was then that it went through a series of organisational transitions. First the Aqueous Nasal Sprays were shed (as different sites were involved in this to the other dose forms), and then Dry Powders (which used the Diskus device), which as an emerging dose form became a separate group.

The Inhaled Products TLG then rebranded itself as the Aerosol Manufacturing Excellence Forum (AMEF) covering the Ventolin, Becotide, Seretide and Flixotide product range. There was a desire to change its way of working and deliver more output, particularly in conjunction with the fledgling Lean Six Sigma programme. However in reality 80–90 per cent of the AMEF meetings involved sharing information on current business issues or developments. Although this resulted in sites gaining a better understanding of issues, thus enabling them to deal with them better, little action was taken to change things *directly* as a result of the meetings. The leader's role was strengthened, but he estimated he was only spending 10 per cent of his time on the group, and in practice the group was sustained by three things:

- common products, processes and to a certain extent equipment, leading to common problems;

- a global transition to a non-CFC propellant in the aerosols;

- relationships that had been built up between the participants from the five main aerosol supplying sites.

The relationship (between the Operations Managers) was particularly important in sustaining the community through this period. Production volumes were declining and there was a strong desire for self-preservation. (A decade later three of the five sites no longer manufacture aerosol products, and one has completely closed.) There were some politics, but in general these were left outside the meetings and the group was left to focus on technical issues. One breakthrough moment occurred however when one site admitted it was having capacity issues and agreed to transfer orders to another site.

In the early 2000s a Global Technical Director was appointed who took on leadership of the CoP, partly in response to the lack of time the previous leader was able to devote to the group. He regarded the CoP as a means of achieving his, and the sites', objectives and transitioned the group into a key component of the technical organisation, notching up a series of collaborative successes resulting in clear financial and supply benefits. When problems occurred, the understanding of each other's operations and the relationships that existed enabled time to be saved in achieving a resolution, and in one instance it was estimated that the established relationships saved three weeks work to solve a technical issue. It was a place where things got done – sub-groups were formed when there was:

- global or cross-site benefit;

- a common issue for resolution;

- shared objective from stakeholders.

Setting up these groups delivered benefit through:

- the level of technical input;

- a raised awareness/priority;

- development of a solution which could be used by all.

But clear ownership within the CoP needed to be ensured.

Another key change was the awareness that the group needed to generate outputs to keep up its profile and make stakeholders aware of what it was doing. These outputs were identified in the group's charter and an ongoing communication process was implemented to make them visible. They included:

- a dashboard of the progress with the four top priority projects was completed during every meeting then e-mailed;

- a periodic update on all AMEF projects was issued;

- 1:1s were held by the AMEF Leader with the senior executive responsible for Manufacturing and the relevant Site Directors;

- members communicated meeting outputs/achievements to their site management teams and production teams.

The resultant stakeholder recognition of the benefits of the CoP promoted its use as its expertise was seen to work for all involved.

Besides the technical and operational improvements that the CoP made, and the issues that it helped to resolve, it was very much seen as a hub of expertise. At the end of one meeting (they were held three or four times a year) a new Operations Manager at one of the sites said:

> This meeting has been the best start I could have had in my job. It would have taken me months to learn what I have learned here in two days.

Despite a 90 per cent focus on Production operations, it was always attended by a representative from R&D. When asked about the value that they got one manager said:

> It's a great opportunity for me to keep up to speed with operational issues, but more importantly to gain feedback on ideas that we have, and projects that are ongoing in Development, with the people who are going to implement them.

The CoP facilitated the rationalisation of manufacture mentioned earlier, and despite the small number of sites involved the group lives on to this day, over 20 years after it started.

A COMMUNITY OF PRACTICE (COP) IN THE CONTEXT OF RATIONALISATION

Another CoP in GSK Manufacturing already mentioned is the Cephalosporin CoP. This started life as a Technical Liaison Group, as did the Aerosol Group, however it had very different dynamics. We have already mentioned the importance of relationship building and this was critical to the successes of the Cephalosporin CoP as David Cunningham, who facilitated the group for a number of years, describes:

> The Cephs CoP was dominated by Barnard Castle (BC) and Verona as the prime Cephs secondary manufacturing sites, and the other sites generally respected their views or evidence. From that I certainly saw that the two prime sites had different strengths, in so far as Verona had very good links with the equipment suppliers (in Bologna) and worked closely with them to develop machines. Conversely BC were stronger in validation of systems, sterility assurance, barriers on the filling machines and so on, and there was a good and 'robust' exchange of views, reasonable understanding, detailed communication and generally good co-operation between the two sites, despite the element of competition.

There was a transition in the group following the Glaxo Wellcome/SmithKline Beecham merger in 2001 when production of Cephalosporins was rationalised against a background of declining volumes. All sterile production was allocated to Verona and non-steriles to Barnard Castle with production at all other sites scheduled to cease. David continues:

> The transfers of products (of stock keeping units – SKUs) and the transfer of all the associated information went reasonably well and this was really about professional and individual contacts, built on the contacts made between the two sites at the CoP. There was also good co-operation and focus on equipment choice. For instance Barnard Castle adopted the Giloway sterilising tunnels which had been standard at Verona for many years before. Barnard Castle progressed barriers for sterility assurance (non-intervention) which Verona copied. Both sites worked on a change to moulded vials rather than tubular vials, where the glass was heavier and the vials were fractionally more expensive, but worth it as it dramatically reduced the risk of breakage during processing and during transit to the customer. They both adopted

pre-washed, pre-sterilised rubber plugs for the vials. These changes and rationalisations progressed relatively smoothly. Barnard Castle led the testing and validation and Verona were happy to accept the work carried out. Underlying the informal contacts and discussion was the documentation to which both had contributed.

Again this illustrates how personal relationships, laced with a degree of pragmatism, sustained the community through difficult business conditions and enabled business objectives to be achieved. We shall now look at an example where, through the introduction of structure and processes, an informal group was transitioned into a productive CoP.

THE AVANDIA COMMUNITY OF PRACTICE (COP) – FROM A TALKING SHOP TO A HUB FOR TECHNICAL ISSUES AND IMPROVEMENT

John Riddell recounts his involvement with the Avandia CoP:

In late 2006, I picked up that two meetings had been held between eight sites manufacturing the Avandia tablet product range (2006 sales £1.6bn) where there were significant technical challenges. Sitting in on the next meeting I observed that whilst there was good knowledge sharing (resulting in meetings not completing the agenda) there were few clear actions being agreed. The opportunity existed to improve the organisation and structure of the group to deliver clear results, and the potential for benefits from increased collaboration, that is, transition it into a CoP.

I took on de facto leadership of the group and sponsorship was obtained to transition the group. Relationships were built with the key members of the group (Site Technical Directors from USA, Canada and Spain) with them creating a leadership team for the CoP. The following actions were taken to transition the group:

- *the group relaunched through a meeting involving 30 staff, with the VP present;*
- *three telecons were then held with the leadership team. Through the meeting and telecons a project list was established and prioritised, and a categorised membership list established;*
- *regular community teleconferences were set up, and a formal communication process to involved staff not attending the face-to-face meetings was established;*

- *stronger links were built with the Avandia Product Strategy group and the overlapping databases of the two groups merged.*

During this period the CoP addressed a number of technical issues with the manufacturing processes, one of which resulted in a saving of $2.7m per annum. It also worked to align the processes between the sites, thus improving regulatory compliance and security of supply. The need for a permanent leader was identified and after a period of four months in which two group members took on the role on a part-time basis the VP appointed a full-time leader. Following CoP Leadership training he took over and continued to build from these new foundations.

Conclusion

The three aspects of Knowledge Management discussed in this chapter:

- the management of product and process knowledge over the lifecycle of the product;

- product transfer;

- CoPs;

and also Good Practice Transfer (discussed in the next chapter) should be considered as fundamental components of a Knowledge Management strategy for any significantly sized pharmaceutical manufacturing organisation.

They are also very applicable to today's manufacturing environment. As we have described, managing product and process knowledge has a new importance due to the incorporation of ICH Q10 into GMP guidelines. Product transfer is more critical with an increasingly fragmented development pipeline and complex supply chain. CoPs are needed to link together organisation where central (co-ordinating) resource has been cut and where more complex manufacturing and supply means alignment and collaboration are critical. Good Practice Transfer helps to ensure that opportunities are not missed as individual business units are 'leaned' and become more focused and 'heads down' on delivering their objectives.

In the next chapter we consider how Knowledge Management plays a part in other business functions of a pharmaceutical company, beyond the R&D and Manufacturing groups.

Chapter 6

Functional and Commercial Areas

Introduction

In this section we look at the areas that help make a pharmaceutical company function, aside from the R&D, Manufacturing and Technical areas covered in the previous chapters. We explore the practices that exist, and those that might, in these areas of work that have a strong application across many business sectors in addition to the Pharmaceutical Industry.

Typical examples of these areas are Human Resources, Procurement, Quality, Finance, Logistics, Engineering/Projects, and Health & Safety.

Generally these functions are distributed across different and often global company locations. Alignment, integration, working as one team and a culture of improvement are critical success factors in helping to drive the internal supply chain of the company. Marketing and Sales, as the customer-facing components of the company, have some different operational challenges, as we shall see later.

If we consider these critical success factors there are four levels of integration that help to address them across the organisation:

- connecting people – so that they can help and support each other;

- connecting people – in order to share ideas and improvements;

- building collaboration – working together on tasks, projects and common issues;

- CoPs – collaborating over the long term to improve, innovate and build capability.

We will consider each of these in turn.

Connecting People to People to Get Help and Advice

We described the importance of the People component of our KM Framework in Chapter 1, where effective Knowledge Management strategies put people at their core. We consider the cultural and behavioural aspects of implementation in Chapter 7, but here we consider the simplest component of Knowledge Management associated with people, that of 'connecting'.

Since the early days of Knowledge Management, 'Yellow Pages' (also called 'White Pages' or 'Expertise Location Systems') have been considered as a first step for connecting people. These can serve a useful function, but the context of the organisation (that is, will useful connections be made that would not have happened anyway) needs to be considered carefully. The method of generation of the expertise data (manual or automatic) and how this will attain a high degree of completion and credibility is a key factor. This is a good example of an area where an analysis of how a potential project might fail and taking remedial action might be useful. The Lean Six Sigma tool Failure Mode Effect Analysis (FMEA) is valuable in this situation.

The following two case studies illustrate the extremes in connecting people to people. The first involves the introduction of an IT system that went beyond simply enabling the location of expertise, and the second demonstrates that, in the right context, a personal networking approach can suffice.

CASE STUDY – PEOPLE CONNECT

At the start of the GSK Manufacturing KM programme, a small team was established to develop two systems as IT enablers. One was Opentext's Livelink, a Document Management system, which at that time enabled documents to be created and accessed companywide for the first time. The second system was a proprietary system called 'Tacit' which was customised and internally branded as People Connect.

People Connect was a success despite several critical drawbacks. Firstly, it was not recognised as a Corporate System, that is, it was a 'local' Manufacturing system, thus was not fully supported by IT. Secondly, its use was voluntary and only promoted through the efforts of the KM team. Key principles were:

- a user had to create a profile giving information about their expertise and experience;

- the user could join 'Communities', which became focal points for questions on a subject;

- a question could be posted on People Connect by a user, and the system would search for existing answers;

- if these answers were not adequate, People Connect could be asked to provide a list of users whose profile, coupled with any answers they had previously provided, suggested that they might be able to help;

- the user could then choose from the list of experts, and People Connect would send them an e-mail with the question;

- when the experts received the e-mail it would contain a link back to People Connect for the provision of an answer, which would then be added to the database.

People Connect required ongoing management to ensure that answers (and questions) retained on the system were useful and relevant. This was achieved through the system developing into 100 plus subject (and sub-subject) areas to which champions (or moderators) were assigned. They had various powers, including the deletion of answers and Q&A dialogues, in order to reduce the amount of non-value adding material. Sometimes major reviews were required, for instance when organisational changes resulted in Communities being abandoned!

Tacit, as a commercial product, became discontinued and unsupported several years after implementation as a result of a takeover of the provider, and as a result was ultimately withdrawn from use in GSK. However, in its time it was a clear success as the number of users registered on the system grew linearly for seven years, and at the time that the system reached the end of its life there were 22,000 answers logged.

The main use of People Connect came from support functions. Site-to-site links and site-to-centre links through People Connect were also a great source of help and advice. In one person's case it dramatically changed the way in which he worked, as we describe next.

How People Connect changed the provision of analytical support

A key part of the Analytical Support Manager's role in Central Quality was to help resolve the technical issues that arose with analytical testing encountered at sites. These were usually requested by e-mail, and often different sites were asking the same question in a different way necessitating individual responses. Initially a sceptic of People Connect, the Analytical Support Manager was persuaded to put some commonly asked questions onto the system together with a 'standard' answer. As queries on these subjects came in he referred people to the Q&A and gave them the opportunity to add to it if further clarification was required.

With further encouragement to his site contacts to put questions on People Connect rather than send them to him by e-mail, the Analytical Support Manager rapidly became the top answer provider on People Connect with over 300 answers provided. Queries by e-mail shrank to a dribble, and his time spent answering queries was dramatically reduced.

Lessons learned from People Connect

There are three key learnings from the implementation and use of People Connect:

- Whilst the functionality was great, particularly after a series of modifications following its initial use, ultimately the discontinuation of supplier support and the failure to obtain adoption from IT as a Corporate System, resulted in People Connect being unsustainable in the long term. (The IT group in R&D did experiment with another similar system in the early 2000s but this failed to gain momentum and was discontinued.)

- As a result of only a few mandatory fields in users' profiles there was too much discretion over the amount of information about their expertise that people could put on their profile, in a number of cases leading to little or no real information. This led to a lack of realisation of potential, which could have been resolved through a more rigorous registration process.

- There was a lack of examples of success in its use that could be used to gain more sponsorship from senior management. When seeking feedback on the benefit of answers, getting beyond 'helpful' to hard benefits was extremely difficult.

Summary

The main value that emerged from the use of People Connect was its ability to connect people across the network that were working in the same functional areas, and in enabling them to seek help from each other. Whilst Microsoft's SharePoint and Opentext's Enterprise Information Management are capable of providing similar functionality, the feature of experts receiving e-mails with a clear request from an individual for help was powerful and unique at the time.

CASE STUDY – NETWORKING IN THE SMALLER COMPANY – OTSUKA PHARMACEUTICALS EUROPE

Otsuka is a global research and manufacturing company based in Japan, but with no manufacturing in Europe (about 40,000 employees globally, only 400 in Europe). Otsuka Europe is a virtual company, with bulk dosage forms imported into the EU for packaging and batch release by third-party packaging contractors. Otsuka Europe owns several affiliates in the EU, which act as sales and distribution organisations.

The Technical and Quality responsibilities, although quite specific, are thus executed on a quite isolated basis, and opportunities have to be taken to generate the support systems, which aid success. In contrast with previous examples, personal networking is the means to facilitate knowledge flow here as Steven Friend describes:

> Contact with my peers is on an ad-hoc basis. There is an annual global production meeting, which I attend alongside US and other colleagues. It's usually a series of presentations by representatives from various factories, heavily biased on Asia as most of the Otsuka factories are in Japan or other Asian countries. They often talk about how they've overcome certain problems. It's really useful for networking as you get to meet colleagues you deal with but usually only through e-mail. This was particularly valuable last time as there were details about how they were going to supply Europe with certain products in the future, after the contract with the existing company ends as we're taking it back ourselves. So it was good to meet colleagues who were taking on the bulk manufacture in the future.
>
> For most projects I'm looking to get information out of the US as they are ahead of us [with products] and I'm regularly in contact with regulatory, technical and quality people there. There is a discussion

*ongoing to create a much more global QA organisation which does exist
in the clinical part of the organisation, but not the commercial.*

Connecting People – How Knowledge Management (KM) can Enhance the Benefits of Business Improvement Programmes by Increasing Visibility of Activities

All businesses at some point, if not on an ongoing basis, will be looking to make improvements to the efficiency and effectiveness of their operations and services. This is particularly important in the support functions that we focus on in this chapter. The following case studies illustrate the role, in a large organisation, that KM can play in maximising the benefit from improvement activities. The first, although centred on GSK's Manufacturing programme, was hugely important with respect to developing a service culture in the support functions. The second illustrates how the same objective of spreading improvement solutions can be driven in the different environment of a sales force.

CASE STUDY – THE DEVELOPMENT OF A LEAN SIX SIGMA PROGRAMME

At the time of the GlaxoWellcome and SmithKline Beecham merger, GW had initiated a programme called Operational Excellence (OE). This was one of the three components of its 'Strategic Master Plan' for Manufacturing which also comprised of Network Rationalisation and Procurement Excellence (essentially rationalised and collective purchasing). SmithKline Beecham had also been running a continuous improvement programme 'Simply Better Way' for several years.

The Knowledge Management Team was a part of the OE programme, and as such played a key part in sharing projects and learnings in order to deliver maximum benefit. Two phases in the programme where the knowledge needs are different are described here: one during the early stages where there was a need to have the maximum sharing of ideas and to build links between practitioners, and the other where the programme was more mature and knowledge sharing was more targeted, extensive and rigorous.

Knowledge sharing in the Operational Excellence (OE) programme

The OE programme consisted of a top-down implementation of Lean Six Sigma. Around six months after the start of the programme and improvement projects had been initiated at sites across the manufacturing network, it became obvious that there were areas where similar projects were being initiated, or improvements were being pursued in similar operations. A database of all Lean Six Sigma projects was constructed and proactive connections made between sites. This led to the exchange of ideas and knowledge on how to go about projects, the transfer of experience from those who had started earlier, and 'buddying' to work together to solve problems. This facilitation of connections sowed the seeds for Knowledge Management to be included as part of the structure of OE at the merger.

That role of facilitating the sharing of, and collaboration on, Lean Six Sigma projects continued for the next ten years. The principle activities were

- Regional meetings of Site Lean Six Sigma Champions were facilitated in order to develop the culture of knowledge sharing.

- The design and facilitation of 'Knowledge Exchanges' of approaches to common improvements, for example, Plant Changeovers, Packing Line Changeovers, Kanbans. 'Best in class' implementation was shared through 'Knowledge Classes' held via webinars, and reference material was created through the generation of a series of DVDs.

- Continuous work was undertaken to generate a culture of openness and sharing, challenging resistance, and the 'Not Invented Here' syndrome which existed, particularly among the more established sites.

The approach was to work closely with the central OE team and to connect with OE champions at sites, particularly during site visits. This reflected the approach's key role in preventing silo working and maximising the value created from the OE knowledge and expertise across the network. During 2004 data was collected on where knowledge sharing on OE projects between sites had led to further projects that generated savings of £6.8 million in that year.

Knowledge transfer of flagship projects

Following on from the previous case study there were several years in which knowledge sharing in the GSK Manufacturing Lean Six Sigma programme was mainly delegated to the Regional Operations organisations. With the 'low hanging fruit' having been 'picked' it was recognised that opportunities were being missed with the 'big-ticket' projects. This was coupled with a desire to achieve the vision of how manufacturing was to be carried out called 'Future State 1'.

The KM team was asked to support the Lean Six Sigma team in producing a method for rapidly and comprehensively sharing knowledge from 'breakthrough' Lean Six Sigma projects. A successful project to be shared across the network was identified as a pilot for the process. The site which had completed the project was to act as host for a workshop held over two days which built on the principles developed for the Product Transfer process described in Chapter 5. Four sites were invited to attend as primary recipients together with support functions. The workshop was videoed and content captured electronically with the aim of generating a Knowledge Transfer which could be understood and applied by others in the manufacturing network who did not attend.

There were four main components to the agenda consisting of an Orientation describing the case for change at the host site and a visit to see the operation, and three Knowledge Exchange and Capture sessions.

The Orientation described what led the site to initiate the improvement project, that is, the business background/context for improvement and the local operating situation. Performance metrics before and after and other benefits were then described. There was then a visit to see the process/systems in action which provided context and understanding for the remainder of the workshop.

The three Knowledge Exchange and Capture sessions followed the same format using two concurrent processes:

- process–knowledge exchange;
  - donor site presentation;
  - Q&A session – receiving sites and donor site panel;
  - other sites' experiences – receiving sites and others;
  - actionable insights and discussion;
  - what does Good Practice look like?
  - variation needed for different environments;
  - barriers to implementation;

- process–knowledge capture;
  - explicit knowledge identified and put in appropriate repository;
  - tacit knowledge captured on video and by scribes;

With the objective of providing a resource for other sites that will be briefed out through a Masterclass.

The themes for the Knowledge Exchange and Capture Sessions were:

- The Practice – focus on operational practice;
  - how it used to work (pre-project);
  - the change we wanted to make;
  - how it works now.

- The Journey – focus on charting how the change was achieved;
  - the plan;
  - what actually was done;
  - how issues were resolved;
  - if we had our time again …

- The Opportunity – focus on building on the work done;
  - how to sustain;
  - opportunities now created (and future planned work).

Some ground rules were agreed in order to aid the flow of discussion and structure:

- ask clarification questions only during donor site presentation, noting others for later;

- ensure each discussion thread reaches a conclusion;

- avoid bringing forward questions more relevant to a later section.

All the content of the workshop was documented and made available to other sites in the network and a virtual Masterclass was held a few weeks later in order to facilitate the Knowledge Transfer to more sites.

CASE STUDY – TRANSFERRING IMPROVEMENTS ACROSS SALES OPERATIONS

John Hardwick describes how a pull, rather than a push, approach was successful in spreading process improvement in a US Sales Force.

> *We did it in three waves, New Jersey, San Francisco area, and then North Carolina. As we went to subsequent waves, there were a lot of people saying that if that was a solution in New Jersey, then that should be implemented in San Francisco. I said no, let's capture the learnings from New Jersey, let's look at what the problems are in San Francisco and just offer the solutions from New Jersey as a palette of options. 'Here's what somebody else did, we don't know whether this would be good for you, but at least you ought to know what they did.' The main thing that we did was document the solutions very thoroughly. We had standard work for the solutions, which included what the solutions were, and also how to implement them, so you could pick them up and use them if you wanted to.*

John's background is in Manufacturing, and he found some interesting cultural differences between Manufacturing and Commercial:

> *In Manufacturing people were always impatient for rapid progress, so they always wanted to mandate or install solutions that hadn't been self-diagnosed or identified by the people trying to make the improvement, that is, Best Practice Replication push, rather than pull.*

> *Interestingly in Commercial we found some viral transfer as well. We made the solutions from New Jersey available to the guys in San Francisco but we also found that other regions were getting hold of them, one way or the other, and were playing around with them as well. So, an interesting culture in Commercial, they're so competitive, that if they hear about something that is giving another team a competitive advantage then they find ways of getting hold of it, and try to use it themselves.*

Building Collaboration – Working Together on Tasks, Projects and Common Issues

CoPs, which we shall go on to look at in the context of support functions and a flagship Knowledge Management technique, are not the only means of bringing people together to share knowledge and perhaps collaborate on common issues. Our first case study provides an example of how sharing knowledge within a functional area aids the governance process. Cross-functional project teams are also examples of groups that need to build collaboration, and we say a bit more about these in the second case study.

CASE STUDY – NOVARTIS VACCINES AND DIAGNOSTICS QUALITY OPERATIONAL EXCELLENCE (QOE) TEAMS

Novartis Vaccines and Diagnostics have established 12 Quality Operational Excellence (QOE) Teams, for example, stability, deviations, validation, quality control (QC) and compliance, to link together their sites. These usually hold fortnightly teleconferences with one representative from each site and the opportunity for site compliance heads to also dial in. Current issues are covered, for example, a site will feed back on a recent inspection and share the report enabling the participants to identify any particular trends and key topics from the inspectors.

The QOE teams are also forums for seeking help. An example is where an internal standard was brought in for endotoxin testing of components. This presented some challenges as to how it could be implemented. This was discussed in the Compliance group and a direction agreed, resulting in a common solution for all the sites.

As we have seen with CoPs, the right criteria were there for the group. A face-to-face was held to build initial relationships and what came out of this was that everyone had the same issues; everyone wanted it to work, generating a real common purpose and enabling agreement on the key areas of focus. A member of the Compliance Group explains:

> *One of the problems is with time, so if one person says that they've developed something, everyone is keen to buy into that, because they*

are pushed for time and resource, that is, if someone had already done it, they are more than happy to accept it, even if they have ideas about how it could be improved. So there is a good culture of accepting other people's solutions and ideas. There can be resistance with some of the things that come out of Corporate, and this is usually driven by resource constraints as it might be seen that it will take a lot of effort to get it to work. We do have someone from Corporate on the calls, who might say 'You have to do it', or might accept the feedback/concerns and take that back to see what can be done.

Novartis use Sparta's Trackwise system which defines a set process for investigation, evaluation, set dispositions and so on for exploring deviations in conjunction with the Deviation Review Board. The system allows for searches (through key words and fields) of previous incidents so that previous experience and outcomes can be drawn upon, and it gives cross-site visibility. An example of a connection that was made was with a deviation for a filter blockage. The search revealed that with this particular product there were previous deviations with high protein content indicating a link that was then referred to the technical support team.

CASE STUDY – DEVELOPING WORKING PRACTICES TO SUPPORT COLLABORATIVE WORKING IN PROJECT TEAMS

Elisabeth Goodman led a business project some years ago, introducing a collaborative working IT tool that was to be adopted by a few hundred R&D project teams. The project team recognised that, in order for this tool to be effective, it needed to define working practices that would be consistently used from one team to the next. This would make it easier for managers to review information across teams, and for individuals who came in and out of different project teams during the course of their lifecycles. There was an experienced Change Manager on the team and, under her direction, the team was able to successfully engage representatives of various project teams to help it shape and roll out the working practices through a combination of focus groups, pilots, and the sharing of case studies and Success Stories. The working practices the team addressed ranged from Document Management principles (for example, version control and filing structures), to guidelines for managing meetings and actions, and protocols for using chat/messaging systems.

Communities of Practice (CoPs) – Collaborating Over the Long Term to Improve, Innovate and Build Capability

Whilst pharmaceutical companies come in all shapes and sizes, the functions mentioned at the start of this chapter – Human Resources, Procurement, Quality, Finance, Logistics, Engineering/Projects, Health & Safety, Marketing and Sales are endemic in most pharmaceutical organisations. Indeed, the presence, role and processes of some of these functions are prescribed (sic) by the various pharmaceutical regulatory bodies, particularly that of Quality.

Within a company that is distributed across various locations, the opportunities to connect, share, learn and collaborate will exist to different degrees. If one considers the scenario where there is a significant operational spread, these functions will usually have a component with a global role of governance and the development of competency to meet regulatory requirements, or the expectations of the customer. However, whilst a Central Function will interpret requirements and set policy, and provide guidance, the practical implementation is carried out locally.

The role of the local operation will be to:

- comply with internal and external requirements, for example, Quality, Health & Safety, Regulatory;

- train and develop a competent workforce;

- sustain and continuously improve to achieve business objectives.

The role of the Central Function and the local operation are represented in Figure 6.1.

CoPs, which we described in Chapter 1, provide an ideal way to link these two systems as they are:

- a vehicle for functions to carry out their governance role by helping sites to obtain the best advice and experience for compliance – co-ordinated and aligned across the network – to maximise value;

- a way to build capability in key business areas;

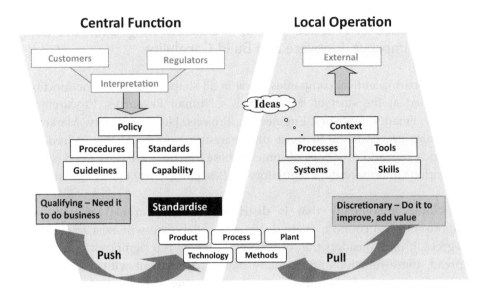

Figure 6.1   Functional leadership and Communities of Practice

- a way for sites to help themselves, and each other, so that they gain knowledge direct from the 'grass roots'.

This CoP approach provides a way for Central Functions to carry out their role (see Figure 6.2), but requires a complete change of mindset as, instead of acting as a route for the transfer of knowledge, they act as a facilitator. The result is that sites gain knowledge directly from their peers, people develop their own skills and competency in their area of expertise, and organisational capability is built. This way of working for functions provides a richer and more sustainable way of achieving objectives.

Here are three case studies from GSK which demonstrate different ways in which CoPs can play a key role in the delivery of functions' objectives:

- how a Logistics department linked internal operations, internal customers and external providers together to improve the distribution of products in Europe;

- how the formation of a CoP was part of a strategy to address a lack of statistical capability in Manufacturing;

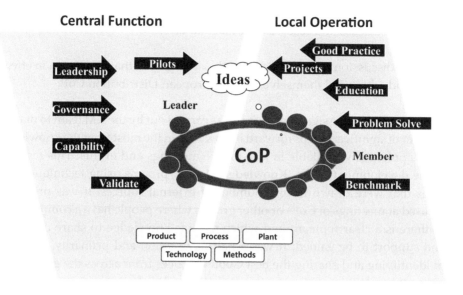

Figure 6.2 How Communities of Practice link Central Functions and Local Operations

- how, arising from a small meeting to co-ordinate Lean Six Sigma projects, a Lean Laboratory CoP grew to become a key component of developing excellence in laboratories.

CASE STUDY 1 – LINKING THE SUPPLY CHAIN TOGETHER – HOW USING A KNOWLEDGE SHARING APPROACH HELPED A LOGISTICS FUNCTION

The Logistics function had arranged several meetings of staff from Distribution Centres across Europe (Pharma and Consumer) with Logistics Service Providers representatives from manufacturing sites and local marketing companies.

They got together three times a year to:

- share industry news;

- share Good Practices;

- present and discuss continuous improvement projects;

- work as a team to address common issues;

•   discuss and resolve issues face-to-face.

Through discussion with the KM team they recognised that they were, in effect, a CoP and rebranded themselves as the European Distribution CoP.

At the same time significant work was carried out by the KM team to make a number of significant steps forward in how to gain the most from the knowledge that is potentially available in face-to-face meetings and events. This resulted in the development of the 'Knowledge Market' process using techniques and ideas that were drawn from a number of external sources. It was primarily focused at meetings of CoPs or other groups where people have a common role or there is a clear topic around which there is knowledge to share or advice and support to be gained. It was a half-day session and primarily consisted of identifying and sharing the best Good Practices from across the group, and generating advice and ideas on issues that attendees had raised.

It was adopted by the European Distribution CoP, immediately became a success and was adopted as the main component of their meeting, demonstrating that when the right criteria and environment are present, KM processes can significantly add value (as opposed to people finding their own way with knowledge sharing).

CASE STUDY 2 – STATISTICS – BUILDING ORGANISATIONAL CAPABILITY THROUGH A COMMUNITY OF PRACTICE (COP)

In 2004, following concern over the specialist statistical support for the Lean Six Sigma programme, the President of Manufacturing appointed a Global Head of Statistics and sponsored a meeting of approximately 40 statisticians and Six Sigma experts and relevant managers to address the lack of capability in the area. It became evident during the meeting that a CoP would be the ideal approach and the idea was broached. The new Head of Statistics was easily convinced; indeed he later expressed the view that a CoP was the *only way* through which he could have achieved his objectives. After a brief period of convincing key stakeholders, the CoP was launched – with a leadership team and a number of specialist sub-groups established.

A conference for those involved in statistics was held in each of the two following years, and these conferences had a tremendous impact in creating networks among the statisticians and Six Sigma experts. The result was that those statisticians, who were perhaps alone in their role at a location, gained a support network and the means to get practical help. It also brought the individual statisticians closer together and enabled them to work with a more common voice.

The Statistics CoP grew to 240 members by the end of 2007, with statistical capability across the whole organisation harnessed into an effective community. One of the successes was that the IT project manager for new statistical software became an integral member of the leadership team. He created a software sub-group through which he gained feedback on requirements and system performance. This was key to the successful introduction of the software.

The growth, activities and the value that it gave to its members and the organisation reflects the opportunity, given the right mindset, for a CoP to lead the development of functional capability in an organisation. (Unfortunately the story does not have a happy ending as the Head of Statistics retired in 2007, and the new incumbent did not have the same approach, so the CoP quietly died.)

CASE STUDY 3 – LEAN LABORATORY COMMUNITY OF PRACTICE (COP) – FROM AN AD-HOC MEETING TO A GOVERNANCE ROLE

Shortly after the initiation of a Lean Six Sigma programme, it was recognised that a number of manufacturing sites were initiating similar projects. Foremost in this were projects to introduce Lean principles into laboratory testing. The first seeds of the community were sown in a meeting of Lean Six Sigma Black Belts who came together to share the status of their projects one evening at a Heathrow hotel. It was agreed that there would be benefit in a deeper sharing, so a one and a half day meeting was held at a site a few months later with Black Belts from ten sites attending. Beside the huge value gained by those attending there was an awareness that many more sites would probably be looking to go down the same route. A key output was a 'blueprint' of the basic steps of Best Practice for achieving a 'Lean Laboratory'.

At this point the Quality function became interested and progressively took on a leadership role of what had now clearly become a CoP. A year later, with a number of sites having already gained major benefits from implementing Lean Laboratory projects, a conference was organised and attended by 55 staff from 26 sites. The conference was designed to enable staff to share their experiences and learnings with others who were engaged in, or who wanted to do a project; and also to work together to accelerate improvements further. The three-day conference included a day spent visiting laboratories that had completed Lean Laboratory projects. A sub-group took on an update and enhancement of the blueprint.

During the following year, the focus was on rolling out Lean Laboratory at a regional level, engaging laboratory managers via regional quality meetings. A package of information was made available to Lean Six Sigma Site champions for use in a pre-project workshop. This included the blueprint, presentations and videos, and enabled sites to utilise existing knowledge as much as possible, before embarking on their own improvements. Data was also collected from across the network of projects planned, in progress or completed along with contacts and so on.

A survey was then undertaken to assess the value that the various Knowledge Management approaches and tools were bringing to what was now becoming a global implementation. Beyond the usual feedback of 'helpful', at the larger-sized sites, use of the CoP's knowledge was quoted as saving between ten and 20 days of labour when running a Lean Laboratory project. Whilst this is a significant saving, this can be regarded as a conservative estimate, as it would not include waste (in time, money and effort) avoided and improvements to the effectiveness of the project. More in-depth analysis of the responses revealed that, although geographical locations and cost can act as a barrier to visiting other sites, where this was done it proved the best method of gaining knowledge to help with a project.

The CoP then went into a period of lower activity, and perhaps decline, for two years, primarily due to the following:

- the person who put himself forward as leader turned out not to be sufficiently focused on the role, thus the community suffered from a lack of drive, presence and direction;

- there was a feeling amongst some stakeholders and those involved early on that the CoP 'had done its job' (in generating the blueprint and a database through which people could contact each other). In addition the early stage 'experts' had mostly moved onto other projects and were unwilling to be repeatedly responding to queries from sites now picking up the baton.

It was at this point that the Vice President responsible for providing a central technical support service recognised that an opportunity was being missed and took on the task of reviving the Community:

- a major change of scope was made with the objective of being available to all 2,700 bench chemists and microbiologists within Manufacturing;

- its purpose was to support the application of business efficiency with the QA and QC laboratories, on all 80 sites;

- it linked into a number of key projects relevant to laboratory operations, but maintained its strong foundation in Lean Six Sigma;

- two Vice Presidents were identified to be sponsors;

- rather than have one full-time leader, the leadership role was shared between three staff that would assign one-third of their time and each have a different focus. This created the opportunity for development of these staff through the role, and avoided the commitment of one individual;

- a core team of 14 was assembled who would become the hub of the CoP;

- CoP ways of working and activities were identified;

- six business-driven objectives were identified and agreed. Included was a new version of the Blueprint with a change in emphasis from use of Lean Manufacturing tools to Six Sigma tools, and a new section on the design of laboratories.

The relaunch revived the CoP, it became very active and a part of the landscape in the Quality/Analytical area. The following quote from one of the co-leaders, could be reflective of many CoP Leaders:

> *A lot of hard work has gone in, and continues to go in, from both the Lean Laboratory leadership team and the core team. IF we have been successful, it has not been luck, or an accident!*

Conclusion

In this chapter we have described how the components of Knowledge Management, set out in our Framework and described in Chapter 1, extend beyond the focal points of R&D and Manufacturing to the other functions present in a pharmaceutical company. The particular elements of connecting people to enable human resources to be used effectively, share ideas and improvements and ensure alignment, and building collaboration across the organisation stand out as ways in which KM can deliver benefit.

In the next chapter we return to our KM Framework and discuss the enablers that are critical to driving and sustaining KM.

PART III
Knowledge Strategy

Chapter 7

Supporting and Sustaining Knowledge Management

Introduction and the Consideration of Culture

We introduced our KM Framework in Chapter 1 (Figure 7.1). This consists of what we believe are the core components of Knowledge Management: the mental models that provide the common language around KM in the organisation; the business goals that provide the context for KM activities, and the measures (or key performance indicators (KPIs) that determine their success; the sources of knowledge (Content Management and People) and the tools, processes, technology and capabilities that facilitate their flow. We cover the right hand side of the model, the enablers, in this chapter.

Our own experience, and that of many experts and practitioners in Change Management, is that there are several key determinants or enablers of success for driving and sustaining any kind of strategic and organisational change. Since the adoption and integration of Knowledge Management as a way of working within the Pharmaceutical Industry is in itself a form of strategic and organisational change, these enablers will also be key to its success. Here then is what we believe are those enablers:

- a clear vision of the outcomes and benefits of a KM strategy;

- a solid cascade of strong sponsorship, prioritisation and role modeling from the CEO downwards;

- motivators for the desired behaviours and culture, including the organisation's performance management system;

- processes to demonstrate the benefits gained and to build traction within the organisation, for example, Quick Wins, sharing case studies and success 'stories';

A Framework for Knowledge Management

Components

Change Enablers

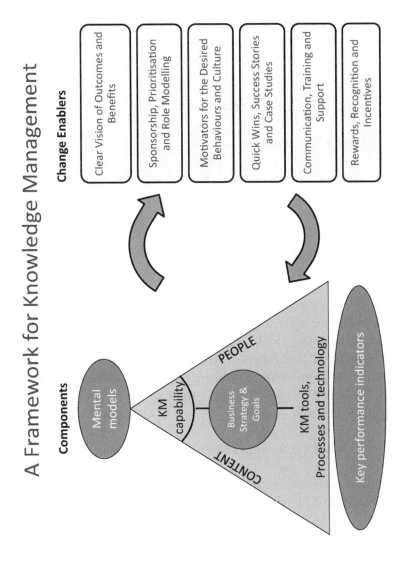

Clear Vision of Outcomes and Benefits

Sponsorship, Prioritisation and Role Modelling

Motivators for the Desired Behaviours and Culture

Quick Wins, Success Stories and Case Studies

Communication, Training and Support

Rewards, Recognition and Incentives

Mental models

PEOPLE

KM capability

Business Strategy & Goals

KM tools, Processes and technology

CONTENT

Key performance indicators

Figure 7.1   A framework for Knowledge Management

- a Communication, Training and Support strategy to facilitate the new processes and ways of working;

- cultivation of desired behaviours through rewards, recognition and incentives.

Before considering these enablers it is important to consider whether culture (the values, attitudes and beliefs, behaviours, capabilities and general environment to support the new way of working) is something separate from any of the above determinants of success, or if it is in fact a product of all of them. Does the introduction of organisational change involve changing the culture or is it a question of effectively taking it into account? Our view, supported by Katzenbach, Steffen and Kronley (Katzenbach, Steffen and Kronley 2012), is that to be effective in introducing sustainable change, we must take account of the existing culture: it is a question of finding the 'open door' that only needs a slight push, or better still that draws us in! At the same time, it is inevitable, and desirable, that the change will result in a shift of culture: behaviours, mindsets and working practices will need to be altered, and these are all key components of cultural change.

An example of this cultural consideration is the 'Not Invented Here' syndrome: the reasons that people put forward for not adopting or even considering the benefits of a practice employed elsewhere. This can be because people are fearful of accepting that someone else has generated a Good Practice. Or it may be because they prefer to come up with their own ideas and solutions, or this is what they are rewarded for. In this instance there is work to be done, mostly by senior management, to change attitudes and motivators. Going straight into a Knowledge Transfer process would be a waste of time! However once a receptive and co-operative culture is established, techniques that develop collaboration, such as CoPs, come into play. Thus it is important to establish how the existing culture affects the starting point for the vision of Knowledge Management and what change in culture is inherent to the vision.

Trust is an important aspect of the culture for Knowledge Management. The potential barriers imposed by a 'blame culture', concerns about confidentiality and lack of trust are key issues to address in order to drive the right behaviours for effective KM. People's comfort with sharing what they know can be affected by the predominant culture of the organisation, and also by insecurity during significant organisational change. This is illustrated by the following example.

OVERCOMING ISSUES OF TRUST AND CONCERNS ABOUT CONFIDENTIALITY

Where trust is not present, things will just not happen. This was Tony Murabito's experience when, fresh from driving the Knowledge Management strategy at what was then SmithKline Beecham, he tried to do the same at Transkaryotic Therapies (now Shire). He did it without CEO involvement, and initially there was not a good sense of trust. People would ask: 'Why should I share information? What am I going to get out of it? I'll just lose out of it.' Tony and his team put in technology and processes to support Knowledge Management, but without addressing the cultural barriers, KM initially did not get off the ground.

In this chapter we use extracts from the case studies that we've described more fully elsewhere in the book, together with some additional examples from our own experiences, to explore each of the enablers for driving and sustaining Knowledge Management in the Pharmaceutical Industry.

A Clear Vision of the Outcomes and Benefits of a Knowledge Management Strategy

Knowledge Management requires effort, resources and, as it is a long-term change, the will to see it through. An organisation is not going to commit and maintain its commitment unless it has a clear vision of the outcomes and the benefits that KM will bring. As our first paragraph in Chapter 1 stated, every approach and application is unique: there is definitely no 'one size fits all'. The vision needs to be developed by each individual company from inputs provided by this book and many other sources. The company culture and the views of senior managers will affect the ability to get started with KM, with views ranging from requiring a business case with returns on investment, to a simple leap of faith, that is, 'it's the right thing, so let's just do it!'

ARTICULATING AND DEMONSTRATING BUSINESS BENEFITS

In Chapter 1 we put the linking of KM to business strategy and goals at the centre of our KM Framework. There is also a need for an overarching Knowledge Management strategy: to link different, common and overlapping business benefits from Knowledge Management into an overall cultural change. However, as Lee Harland has found, it can be difficult in big organisations for different departments to think holistically for example, outside their own internal and external information requirements, making it difficult to define business benefits:

> It is critical to push the onus for defining this back onto the budget holder – asking them 'what is it you would like to see', 'what would you like to be the outcome of this'? There is a LOT you can do with technology these days, but technology developed in isolation from the real problem is not going to help. You need to understand what can help people first and foremost and then use that.

With the somewhat intangible nature of the benefits of KM, and the potential lack of understanding by users of what KM can deliver, a 'chicken and egg' situation can develop. That is, the benefits of KM cannot be adequately demonstrated without implementing it, and approval to implement cannot be gained without proving the benefits. Often the benefits are intangible, for example, 'it'll be easier to find stuff' – so what? It is very hard to find benefits that are really clear cut. But all scientists know the pain of not being able to access the right information, documents and data at the right time.

This is echoed by Stephen Clulow's experience. He and teams he has worked with have spent a lot of time working with senior executives, explaining KM approaches and the benefits. Stephen has found that the benefits can be very difficult to articulate in a way that makes a strong business case for KM.

> It can be hard to get senior management buy-in. They can be focused on cost- and time-savings and increasing Investigational New Drug (IND) filings. And this is the correct focus. Promoting KM with arguments that centre on improving collaboration is too abstract for them. By structuring justifications to include financial and non-financial benefits the business cases become more understandable and more compelling. Advocating incremental implementations can be very useful. It is easier to get senior management buy-in and it generates real data that can be used to support business cases for expansion. In one instance the Head of R&D became a supportive senior sponsor, and so we were able to roll KM out incrementally to research first, collect feedback through surveys, and indicate savings of more than $3 million in the first year alone. That hard figure made it much easier to then cascade KM through the rest of the organisation including commercial, HR, and so on.

This approach enabled the eventual articulation of knowledge benefits in financial terms. Others have tried to translate knowledge assets more directly into financial value – a perspective that Matthew Loxton also favours. He suggests that knowledge could be perceived as a form of currency – a financial asset:

> What a CFO [Chief Financial Officer] does for cash and tangible assets, a CKO [Chief Knowledge Officer] would do for knowledge and intangible assets. The issue is that it is vital to trace backwards from how the firm sees itself and how it makes its money, and then find the processes and activities and roles that cause this to be successful.

Whether the person responsible for KM is a CKO or someone else, this cause and effect analysis of how an organisation achieves its financial goals would enable it to identify and address the gaps that need to be filled in terms of knowledge creation and curation. Matthew also suggests that an organisation could identify any non-value added knowledge activities and assets and make an informed decision on what to do with these. In some cases, there may be knowledge assets that could be usefully sold off or spun out.

A way to garner support for KM is through carrying out a pilot or pilots, and this is usually successful if the pilot has a short timescale, requires only a small budget or resource, has a business impact, has a sound connection with the forward vision, and its benefits are seen to be scalable.

If credibility is not established early on, this can result in creating a mountain to climb, as one of our interviewees relates from an implementation in one sector of the business:

> When you talk to people about KM the overall reaction is, I'm afraid, that we got our fingers burnt with that approach. I remember our conversations five to six years ago, leadership just don't get it, they think that it's all about the systems, and if you've got a repository then you've got KM, and they don't really think about the people side of it. They haven't really got the roles and responsibilities clear about how does an organisation retain knowledge, how do you maintain it and propagate it down through new people coming into new roles and so on. So I still think that it's seen as a 'slippery bar of soap', and there are some things that have been understood as successful, for example, CoPs. There's not much appetite for talking about KM per se.

> *We're endeavouring to not make the same mistakes in other areas of the*
> *business, but at the same time I'm telling people 'don't throw the baby*
> *out with the bathwater' and that KM has the potential to bring a lot*
> *of value if we don't build a monolith around the systems. I think that*
> *there is also a huge psychological element to it. Having been involved*
> *in a different business area for three years, there's definitely an element*
> *of how you present the knowledge to people.*

The following case studies illustrate an aspect of Knowledge Management, making connections between people, in relation to organisational goals for innovation and for delivering tangible outcomes.

PROVIDING OPPORTUNITIES FOR SERENDIPITOUS KNOWLEDGE SHARING AND IDEA GENERATION FOR INNOVATION

More powerful than any organisational structure, is the ability to serendipitously share insights and ideas with others due to the casual social interactions allowed by sheer geographical proximity. It is something that many of us will have experienced at some time in our lives at the coffee machine, 'water cooler' or in hallway conversations within our organisations: that casual conversation that has helped us to address a problem, find a new person to approach, plant the seed of a fresh idea to explore. Serendipitous knowledge sharing is also something that the increasingly ubiquitous adoption of organisational 'open plan' and 'hot desking' layouts seeks to promote.

Pfizer has actively harnessed this internal social interaction for the generation of new ideas to address business problems, as in their 'Idea Farm' described in an IBM paper in 2009 (IBM 2010), and in their 'Innovation Communities' presented at an American Society for Quality (ASQ) conference in 2012 (Goncalves 2012) . The Innovation Communities were launched in 2009 and, at the time of the ASQ presentation, approximately three years later, had more than 12,000 ideas submitted. The Communities worked on the principle of the 'long tail of innovation': that the people furthest from the originating problem, the tail, are more likely to come up with more, and more diverse ideas – the 80 per cent of Pareto's law. Their approach relied on a combination of the power of the internet, and the strength of networks and teams to discover ideas and to test them out.

Sandra Ward's KM experience included working with an organisation that had introduced a global internal innovation approach. A small-staffed innovation centre, supported by senior management including the CEO and with access to company funds, had been established. The centre encouraged staff to track external possibilities and managed a global idea bank to stimulate idea generation across the entire value chain. Individuals or teams could submit an idea and cross-discipline innovation was actively encouraged. A regular competition for ideas was open to all employees and staff participated in voting on their choices for projects to progress.

At the time that Sandra was involved, the team was going through a second iteration of inspecting ideas:

> *They were holding a boot camp with internal and external technical and business experts to assist in the development of business cases and in coaching on their presentation to a 'Jury' of Senior R&D executives. Successful proposals were awarded funding as projects. Several development projects were currently ongoing. This example shows how an innovative culture can be created in parallel with the formal structure of the organisation, and how ideas based on expert knowledge can emerge from any level of the organization if a process exists to encourage, identify and support them.*

A Solid Cascade of Strong Sponsorship, Prioritisation and Role Modelling From the CEO Downwards

If Knowledge Management initiatives are to be successful, and indeed receive the budgets necessary for their initiation and maintenance, they must at some point become a mandated component of the organisation's overall strategy, with senior management support. However, as we have already discussed at length, KM involves a change of culture and new ways of working at an individual, team, department and corporate level, and thus will not work through a 'go do it' approach. Knowledge Management requires sponsorship through funds and resource, role modelling behaviours and setting expectations of the same behaviour from others, recognition, and support to overcome the frequent 'we don't have the time for this' reaction.

SPONSORSHIP

At GSK, the President of Manufacturing, David Pulman, was a strong supporter of the Knowledge Management programme and used Town Hall meetings and site visits to reinforce his message. This is a typical example of the nature of his support:

> *Our sites and functions must work together in the face of the common threat from generics and other competitors. Sites are not competing against each other; collectively we have a vast store of knowledge in our network that is a resource for all sites.*

Frank van Amsterdam's team's Chief Information Officer encouraged and supported their work with a Knowledge Management tool 'GSK Search' by periodically endorsing it at public events. In addition, as their IT management team represented the whole R&D end-to-end process, from early to late stage R&D, rather than being focused on individual disciplines such as discovery or clinical, they had a strong influence in breaking down silos in the use of the tool.

Schlumberger (an oil and gas services company) have a widely recognised CoP programme. It was stimulated by their Chief Executive going to a particular external meeting and realising that other people were putting in mechanisms to bring people doing similar roles together. He went back, set up a team, appointed someone to lead it, and the function of the Chief Knowledge Officer (CKO) – and many years later it's still winning prizes.

However, the absence of this sponsorship can be devastating as the following case study demonstrates.

Case study

A division of an organisation initiated a KM programme in the late 1990s when it was new and consultancies like Cap Gemini and Anderson were driving it, a recent publication by Nonaka and Takauchi (Nonaka and Takeuchi 1995) had stimulated interest, and tacit and explicit knowledge had come to the fore. All of this indicated the time was right to introduce KM.

The team interviewed hundreds of people, and produced asset maps and strategy documents. It was audacious, with big goals and a lot of enthusiasm from within the division, and for a time it was a cult, complete with branded T-shirts. It did produce some very useful insights, especially in terms of recognising the assets in people's heads and in teams.

However, senior executives were fairly dismissive and, with a change in senior management in the Division the KM programme disappeared almost overnight. Without a champion or champions at a senior level able to influence and gain support from their colleagues, the drivers for change disappear.

THE VALUE OF BOTTOM-UP BUY-IN

Whilst any new way of working requires top-down sponsorship to be successful, it also requires buy-in from every level of the organisation. The most successful change initiatives are therefore also driven 'bottom-up', by those within the organisation who are actually doing the work: designing and delivering the processes, products and services that are at the heart of what the organisation delivers. Any KM strategy thus has to focus on winning their hearts and minds as well as securing commitment from the top.

John Davies believes that Knowledge Management, in the form that he is now seeing it, is a 'person-to-person' discipline. He also believes that replication of knowledge between teams works best as a 'bottom-up' or 'grassroots' approach rather than a 'top-down' one. This is something that he is also experiencing in other business sectors.

On the whole, the experiences that we have described suggest that you actually need both the strategic 'top-down' sponsorship to ensure that Knowledge Management can be driven as a priority, and 'bottom-up' engagement of those involved to ensure traction throughout the organisation.

ROLE MODELLING BEHAVIOURS, SETTING EXPECTATIONS FOR THE SAME FROM OTHERS, AND PROVIDING RECOGNITION

We have described some examples of sponsorship and emphasised that this is not just about 'talking the talk' but it is also about acting in a way that you expect from others. For example, when a senior manager goes to an external meeting or event, they then share the insights they obtained. We shared such an example in Chapter 2. We cite further examples of behaviours that individuals can demonstrate themselves and expect from others in the next section.

In today's pressurised business environment, 'time for KM' remains a key issue, as one of our interviewees describes after introducing Learning Reviews into their Project Management processes:

One (challenge) is time, people saying I haven't got time for this. We're trying to get the message across that this is a core Project Management aspect and needs to be planned in. You wouldn't say I haven't got time to run a risk register so you plan for that. So this is where our Project Management framework should help, and we are putting this into our Project Management templates. We're also looking for our managers to expect teams to have carried these out, but that is still a challenge.

Giving recognition is an important part of sponsorship and it reinforces cultural change. We deal with this in the sixth enabler.

PROVIDING FUNDS AND RESOURCES

No Knowledge Management strategy can be implemented without the appropriate funds and resources. We described the resourcing of a central group to drive and facilitate a KM strategy in Chapter 1 as part of the KM capability component of our framework.

However, funding and resourcing is not just about a central KM team. As we have described, CoPs require the resource of a leader/facilitator, often an expert or manager from the business. Funds may need to be provided separately for CoP meetings (we described the necessity for face-to-face meetings in Chapter 1); particularly as in the current financial climate many business units have had travel budgets paired to the bone. Other similar examples where funds and resource are required are Peer Assists, Learning Reviews, Tacit Knowledge Transfer and Knowledge Retention. Further, there is significant funding and resource implications associated with the Communication, Training and Support enablers we cover later in this chapter, although this may be adequately covered by a KM Central Team combined with IT support.

EFFECTIVE PRIORITISATION OF PEOPLE'S TIME

As Frank van Amsterdam mentions, pressure on people's time comes up repeatedly as a barrier to Knowledge Management. We raise this in this section rather than in others as senior managers are the only ones who can directly affect this: they set objectives and priorities and if they do not make it a part of cascaded objectives, or an inherent component of the task, project or job, then it will be a 'nice to have' and get prioritised out of people's schedules.

This is supported by Helen Chapman who points out that the biggest disincentive to KM seems to be that everyone is so busy. The 24/7 electronic age is both an enabler of knowledge sharing and a barrier in that senior and less senior people just don't seem to have the time to think. And yet:

> *If they are to learn and share let alone structure their thoughts from a people-to-people perspective in a way that can be shared, that needs time. That just does not work if everyone is just far too busy. And we need top-down sponsorship to say it's important to find the time to share for it to happen.*

And this issue of prioritisation of people's time is not new. A 'member spotlight' article (Schurr-Eisinge and Goldstein 2005) in Working Knowledge, the Babson Working Knowledge Research Center's newsletter under the then directorship of Tom Davenport and Larry Prusak, highlighted lack of prioritisation as one of the three main reasons for the absence of a knowledge sharing mindset in drug development at Novartis. (The other two reasons were to do with unwillingness by scientists to show their ignorance, and teams' perception that they were competing for resources and results.) One of the many improvements that the team put in place was to have the Development Management Board role model openness and knowledge sharing through presentations and discussions of lessons learned every two months.

Motivators for the Desired Behaviours and Culture, Including the Organisation's Performance Management System

A very convincing approach for achieving sustainable change (Patterson et al. 2008) begins with identifying the key behaviours that are vital to its success and then works on the influences that will encourage people to adopt them. John Riddell has identified a set of behaviours for successful Knowledge Management implementation and these are shown in Table 7.1 opposite.

Table 7.1 does not aim to be a comprehensive list of the behaviours associated with Knowledge Management. It has deliberately been kept simple in order that the fundamental message may reach everyone in the organisation, and to provide focus for management and assessment.

Our experience, and that of our interviewees, is that Knowledge Management needs the top-down support to get started, training and education to help people learn how to do it effectively, stories and personal experiences

Table 7.1   Knowledge Management behaviours

	Behaviour Description
Personally Demonstrated Behaviours	Seeks knowledge and information from internal and external sources to apply to, or broaden the approach to an issue, task, project or objective. Readily shares relevant information with colleagues and team members. Seeks out and adopts Good Practice from internal and external sources. Values the input of ideas and options suggested by others and acknowledges their contribution.
Influences Others	Creates a culture and puts processes in place to enable the team and others to share information, Good Practices and learnings on a continuous basis to prevent reinventing the wheel and wasted effort. Encourages a culture of re-using practices and ideas from elsewhere. Puts processes in place to enable the team and others to think differently and come up with new solutions and concepts based on learning from others. Builds collaborative working through developing networks and integrating into CoPs to build relationships and maximise the use of the skills, experience and expertise of others for common goals.
Negative Behaviours	Inhibits or prevents the development of new approaches or ideas by shutting out alternatives, e.g. 'We can't do that because' 'We've always done it this way' 'That won't work here' Shows active lack of interest in others' viewpoints, actively discouraging interaction and collaboration across a function or site. Does not share what they're doing, or have done, even when they have knowledge that would prove useful to others.

of the benefits to convince them that it's 'a good thing', and a supportive culture. However, it only really becomes embedded once it becomes part of the way people work: when they've reached that 'unconsciously competent' state of just doing it. This is not something that happens automatically, and this is where integration into the company's performance management system through job descriptions, competency frameworks, progression ladders, annual performance reviews, and so on comes in. Identifying the behaviours, integrating them into the performance management system with different levels identified that enable 'KM Performance' to be recognised and rewarded are key components for a successful KM strategy. The objective is for everyone to be involved and make the change, as David Gurteen puts it in his 'call to arms' (Gurteen 1999).

My personal view is that knowledge sharing starts at the individual. After all – if you are a CEO, a mid-level manager, a receptionist, or a graduate trainee you are still an individual. Each one of us has his or her job, set of objectives and sphere of influence.

If you believe that knowledge sharing is the way to help you; your department; team or organisation meet its objectives then start to practice it within your sphere of influence and encourage others to do the same – 'lead by example'. The higher up the organisation the more influence you have.

KNOWLEDGE MANAGEMENT (KM) CHAMPIONS

What is likely to emerge during implementation is enthusiasts or proponents of KM who can be utilised to champion KM in their sphere of influence. Frank van Amsterdam supports this and feels that the key to spreading the word about Knowledge Management is to get champions to support you and to encourage colleagues. Person-to-person connections are the most effective way to spread new ways of working within an organisation, and it is a well-known fact that some people are better at making connections than others. They are the 'social hubs' that can transcend any formal organisational structure or hierarchy, and they become so through a combination of their more active networking activities, their charisma, the trust that they inspire in others or their 'knowledgeability'.

An example of a champion's activity is given by a contributor:

We've recently introduced Yammer. I've set up an analytical area, and it's moving the conversation from having it 1:1 to "let's have a Yammer". I'm trying to push it heavily as it makes my job a lot easier, and we're up to 131 members of the Analytical community as of this morning, and they'll have visibility of the discussions that are taking place. Currently it's mainly my content on there as I'm pushing it. My goal is to get effective communication with 3,000 analysts across the organisation, and this is one of the ways to do it.

For Martino Picardo, it was his 'knowledgeability', and that of his team of about 40 people working in Amersham's development lab, that determined the success of his first collaborative experience in creating the Technology Transfer opportunity between Amersham and Big Pharma. Martino developed an assay around cholesterol ester transfer protein, and as it was very hard for commercial sales staff to sell a product that was entirely novel and based on very complicated science, he took on the role of Technology Transfer Manager as described earlier. He and his colleagues from Amersham's lab spoke directly to people in AstraZeneca and other companies, either over the phone or in their labs, to understand the problems they were having and to help them understand the value of the technology and how it worked.

However, knowledge champions don't necessarily need to be technical experts. Exhibiting the right behaviours creates role models and David Gurteen reminds us that knowledge sharing is not just about giving. It is about:

- soliciting feedback;

- asking questions

- telling people what you plan to do before doing it;

- asking other people for help;

- asking someone to work with you in some way – however small;

- telling people what you are doing and more importantly why you are doing it;

- asking people what they think; asking them for advice;

- asking people what would they do differently;

- not just sharing information but know-how and know-why.

Fundamentally, sharing is about being more open in your way of work and in your relationships with other people.

KNOWLEDGE CHAMPIONS: CREATED OR FOUND?

Whether intentionally, or purely by chance, some organisations are clearly cultivating 'honest brokers', 'gatekeepers' or 'boundary spanners'.

Michael Koenig recommends that this role is an important adjunct for the success of Lessons Learned in Project Management. He suggests that the role of 'boundary spanners' or 'information gatekeepers' be deliberately assigned to at least one person on the project team. He references the work by Tom Allen where he compared the performance levels of different teams with identical remits, and concluded that it was the use of 'go-to' people that made the difference.

These 'go-to' people are those that you can identify through social network analysis tools, or simply by asking people in a department to identify them: they are the people who have lots of connections, that others go to to find out what is going on. They also connect with each other.

Elisabeth Goodman used this verbal approach to locate suitable champions or 'change agents' in an organisational change project that she was facilitating, and it really did seem to make a difference in helping to engage and involve their colleagues in the overall project.

WHAT'S IN IT FOR ME?

Underpinning the behavioural change discussed in this section is the question of 'What's In It For Me?' People will not change their behaviours and ways of working unless they need to comply, that is, it is included in their role, it will be seen as negative behaviour, or they are motivated through performance goals, rewards, recognition or personal satisfaction. These drivers, and their appropriate use, will vary by company, business unit and individual. There is thus no set way in which to make this change, and this becomes part of the art and challenge of KM.

In the remainder of this chapter we will cover three supporting strategies that help to convince people of the validity of the change and take them through it.

Processes to Demonstrate the Benefits Gained and to Build Traction Within the Organisation – Quick Wins, Sharing Case Studies and Success 'Stories'

Telling people (particularly those senior in the organisation) how KM is working is critical, particularly in the early stages of a strategy implementation. We will consider this through two overlapping areas: that of providing feedback through measures and metrics – generally quantitative; and generating case studies and Success Stories designed to win hearts and minds – generally qualitative. Through this the opportunity should be taken to identify Quick Wins: early successes through initial activities or pilots, which can be used to create a positive environment.

FEEDBACK LOOPS (ON BENEFITS GAINED) TO SUSTAIN SPONSORSHIP

Stephen Clulow used these approaches when he encountered issues of trust and concerns about confidentiality in one company that he worked with. He adopted a strategy that gradually provided open access as more and more people asked for it. As Stephen says:

> *The power came from having an open information system, and users feeding back the benefits they were getting to management – it doesn't start straight-away, it takes time, but you need to maintain the journey and your credibility – you need to have the good Success Stories to tell.*

The organisation did eventually have an 'open to all' policy, which was only waived if there were good regulatory reasons to shut the information down (for example with toxicology or individual human data).

Reduced costs and increased revenue can be two very tangible demonstrations of the benefits of Knowledge Management. They are ultimate 'output' measures of the impact of changing the way the organisation works. Sometimes these results can be calculated relatively easily and quickly as in the examples above, but often the results are far less tangible and can take longer to obtain. It is therefore important for any organisation that is concerned about measuring benefits to identify some 'in-process' metrics that it can monitor during the course of the Knowledge Management programme. These can be quantitative (as with the savings and revenue above) or qualitative.

Lee Harland suggests that Knowledge Management measures could be something as simple as whether people like what is being delivered and whether they use it. At a more tangible level, it may be possible to determine whether people have made a decision as a result of what they learnt from the Knowledge Management deliverable or intervention, or whether it contributed to a product launch. For Lee, it is like a scale:

> *There will be some things that are easy to measure, but have low visibility to shareholders. And there will be some things that will be harder to measure, but have greater visibility to the business.*

QUICK WINS, CASE STUDIES AND SUCCESS STORIES

These are important enabling factors in addition to sponsorship and clear business benefits: there needs to be some tangible contributions to the business, ideally in the form of compelling Quick Wins.

Stephen Clulow's experience of creating an online network of scientists shows what happens when you do not get those tangible contributions to the business. His team's initiative got really good buy-in from the Head of R&D, and he and his team did the classic big launch with lots of publicity, but they got very poor uptake: there were no early or tactical Quick Wins to speak of. So they went back to their customers, the users, and asked them what they liked and did not like, and what they wanted to do and achieve. The team worked with three groups initially to transfer technology from the UK to the US and vice versa. They shared content (experiences and protocols), blogged, asked questions, provided solutions to each other and talked about technology developments for the future.

Stephen Clulow and his team were able to take examples from these three groups and share them throughout the company. They worked from group to group to roll out KM: people gradually joined so that the take up grew organically from a relatively flat initial base to a more exponential curve. Incidentally, this was also a powerful example of what happens when you engage those affected in a 'bottom-up' implementation.

Success Stories and case studies are perhaps two sides of the same coin. Success Stories can be considered as more verbal, focused on the outcome, and designed to fire up the recipient with enthusiasm for a new way of working. At GSK, we had a great example with People Connect (the Expertise Locator/ Q&A system mentioned in Chapter 6) where a question raised received six responses from three continents in two days and resulted in 32,000 Canadian dollars per annum being saved. Case studies can be considered as more likely to be documented and focused on the process, as illustrated by the case studies provided in Chapter 5.

Storytelling is often quoted as a way to get the KM message across. It can be a detailed narrative of past management actions, employee interactions, or other intra- or extra-organisational events that are communicated informally within the organisation. Usually narratives will include a plot, major characters, an outcome and a moral to the story. Our experience is that stories that will have the desired effect on an audience are usually hard to define, and generally drop into the category of Success Stories or case studies that we have already discussed. Given the scientific nature of the pharmaceutical environment, we have been somewhat disinclined to use this technique, and we have not come across its use in this environment.

Ultimately, one of the greatest influences for changing behaviour is when people's peers start to adopt the new way of working, and the benefits become more visible. It is the 'tipping point' as described by Malcolm Gladwell (Gladwell 2000) for change to spread, and one experienced by Frank van Amsterdam. He found that once their online thesaurus (DEX) got some critical mass, people became interested and wanted to take ownership for some of its content – they could see the benefits.

This is where being able to share success becomes so important, as with the example we shared earlier from Stephen Clulow in the exponential growth of the online science community where the 'message' spread through 'word of mouth'. As Stephen says:

> A companywide launch is difficult to manage and runs the risk of a high-profile failure. An incremental approach allows you to experiment to find an approach that works in that organisation. It enables you to generate Success Stories to maintain the momentum and increase the scope of the implementation.

Tony Murabito also experienced this at Cubist, where being able to relay successes, capture and share them was a major driver right from the start. He found that the diverse media available for sharing these stories of success really made for a powerful catalyst of change.

A Communication, Training and Support Strategy to Facilitate New Processes and Ways of Working

Our experience is that people need to be guided and supported in the adoption of Knowledge Management practices and tools, whether that is through the presence of a skilled facilitator for Learning Reviews, collaborative working, or hands-on training and online help in the use of computer systems.

THE NEED FOR TRAINING

We see training as a critical component of a KM strategy, not just in the KM tools and techniques, but in the technology that provides access to explicit knowledge and enables people to connect. Technology has moved forward apace and continues to do so. When new systems or upgrades are introduced, there is a current tendency to rely on people to self-teach. This is short-sighted and cost ineffective, but unfortunately training is usually an easy target when the project budget is being trimmed. You will have the enthusiasts and the 'geeks' who will latch onto, and get excited about new technology, and those who are 'tech savvy' and can pick things up quickly, and these can help with the Quick Wins that we have just described. However, there is a large group of people that derive great benefit from training in the use of new technology, and there are those that will be resistant and need to be cultivated in its use.

This view is supported by Michael Koenig who argues that whereas change programmes and conclusions from the literature tend to focus on sponsorship and senior management support as the most important factors for influencing and changing behaviour, training and education are in fact more important. He cites research by KPMG in the early 2000s on 300 companies that had KM systems in place where almost half of them were regarded as a failure. He points out that although they carried out a detailed analysis, they failed to notice that three of their reasons for failure: lack of user uptake and insufficient communication, lack of time to learn or the system being too complicated, and lack of training were the same thing: a lack of training and user education. Michael goes on to cite an article published about five years ago (at the time of writing) on KM in pharma in Taiwan that had similar conclusions:

> They say that lack of leadership and commitment of senior management has no significant effect on the attention paid to KM, but that employee training and involvement has a high effect on the attention paid to KM (and enhancing company competitiveness). However in the abstract they pay almost no attention to training, yet in the middle of the article they say that that's the one that's had the high impact.

In a 2008 paper (Bartholomew 2008) on the application of Knowledge Management technologies at AstraZeneca and Baxter the author, Doug Bartholomew, quotes Jim Murphy, a Knowledge Management Analyst at AMR Research, an IT research firm in Boston. Murphy acknowledges that how technology is applied in Knowledge Management is only 20 per cent of the problem, 'the rest being a people and a training issue'.

Finally a simple illustration of the point was brought home to us in a discussion with Michael Koenig when we suggested using Skype for a conversation with him, and he said that he didn't know how to use it.

> There are always too many other things to do. If someone offered to spend a couple of minutes showing me I'd be grateful. But if it's left to me I don't know whether it's going to take two minutes or two hours to figure it out, and there's always something that needs to be done now. So expertise location is not complicated, but if someone doesn't show you how to use it, and help you to see how it works. So when someone puts together a proposal for a system, for example, Yammer, the time for the training doesn't get put in the budget, they don't recognise that it's important.

PROVIDING SUPPORT AND FACILITATION

The connection between Knowledge Management, knowledge sharing, Learning and Development is very strong. A key behaviour for Knowledge Management is that people actively share what they have learnt from experience and this is central to Helen Chapman's work with pharmaceutical companies. However, efforts at encouraging people to share what they have learnt can be met with resistance in organisations that do not have the right culture to encourage this, and necessitates the need for a facilitated intervention.

For example, participants' discomfort to talk about what has not worked can be aggravated if there is a 'blame culture' as opposed to active encouragement to learn from mistakes. Helen has found that facilitating Appreciative Inquiry: 'What have we found that works?' is a very productive way of encouraging people to share what they know by encouraging people to talk about what they are good at first, and then explore related topics. She believes that it supports innovation, as well as helping people to surface things that they might not otherwise have thought of:

> If you think about how people's brains are wired in a way like any sort of database or web, then the Appreciative Inquiry route enables you to mine information that people hold within their heads in a way that may not have previously been mined.

Whilst we agree that Appreciative Inquiry is very powerful for the reasons that Helen Chapman gives, learning from what has not worked well is also valuable.

We have worked as objective outsiders to facilitate Learning Interventions consisting of the following steps:

- one-to-one interviews or questionnaires to encourage those involved to talk about what has not worked well, as well as what has worked, and to come up with recommendations on how things could be done differently going forward;

- anonymous collation of the results to draw out the main themes and recommendations;

- review of these results with team leaders to give them the opportunity to reflect upon the implications for their own behaviours and to add their ideas;

- facilitation of a team workshop involving a constructive review of all of the inputs and to identify actions that the team can take forward as a result.

Facilitating knowledge sharing is also important when an obvious intervention is not required. As mentioned in Chapter 4, one company runs a version of David Gurteen's Knowledge Cafés for those involved in development projects. Although these Cafés are going 'quite well', our interviewee highlights that the need for facilitation is clear:

> We want people to be more transparent and not feel afraid about saying 'that went wrong', and 'if I had my time again I would do this, this and this'. In our tightly regulated industry it's difficult for people to open up to things that have gone wrong but it's imperative that we continually learn from mistakes and the Regulators are openly wanting this – its good science – and we have a whole range of technical reviews, CoPs and the knowledge sharing cafés in order to share our approaches and outcomes.

These issues are also encountered within the project teams. Whilst identifying potential risks and finding ways to mitigate them is a key aspect of effective Project Management, there is a mindset that risks are negative, but they are also opportunities. They are in effect something positive: an opportunity to identify an element of the project that, with enough knowledge and foresight, can be mitigated or avoided.

The need to support KM activities in order to sustain them was evident in Elisabeth Goodman's experiences with CoPs for sustaining practitioners in Lean and Six Sigma in R&D. Elisabeth facilitated the establishment of site-based 'lunch and learn' CoPs, which were formed by people who had undergone the equivalent of yellow- and green-belt training in Lean and Six Sigma. They were leading and participating in process improvement projects, and wanted to continue to develop their knowledge and expertise by discussing case studies, sharing Best Practices and through ongoing study of the principles and tools involved.

As well as facilitating culture change, active support is required in the use of technology. During Frank van Amsterdam's work with Documentum he and his team had to educate people to include meta-data, titles, dates and authors in their records. They tried to build prompts into the technology, in the form of pop-up windows, but people would close the windows and ignore the prompts because they did not understand the value of including this information. People also saw adding meta-data as unnecessary work, which conflicted with the pressures on their time for R&D projects. So Frank and his team looked for ways to make the creation of meta-data as automatic as possible, for example, through the use of default data that could be accepted as it was or easily edited. They also found that by focusing on workflow, they could help people make the process fit more seamlessly into their work:

> *Often it's a question of setting up the right workflow so that you can forget about all the documents on the way and just focus on the final repositories for the quality information. If the workflow is part of the system, then it's easier for people to follow and do things the right way.*

Frank also found that people worried about having too sophisticated a search engine, because it would allow others to find confidential information that they wished would rather remain unfound – instead of appreciating that this would enable them to surface these kinds of problems and so take measures (like improved access control) to mitigate risk.

COMMUNICATION

The need for a high level of communication as part of any change programme is well accepted and is inherent in all of the activities in this chapter. Effort is required to get KM on the agenda at Town Hall and senior management meetings, and to publicise activity and Success Stories in corporate communications. At

GSK the central KM team produced a quarterly newsletter which, amongst others, was sent to the Knowledge Managers at all the manufacturing sites who then distributed it locally, enabling a greater reach and the opportunity to add local context.

Cultivation of the Desired Behaviours Through Rewards, Recognition and Incentives

The fragmentation that the Pharmaceutical Industry is experiencing at the present day could itself be having a negative impact on trust and people's willingness to share what they know. Many readers will be aware of the mantra: 'Knowledge is power', and whereas we Knowledge Management practitioners seek to change that mantra to 'knowledge sharing is power' – it is often an uphill task when people's jobs are at risk.

This is a view held by Michael Koenig who believes that people may hoard what they know as a safety net and that pharmaceutical companies therefore have the challenge of encouraging people to share their knowledge when they do not feel secure. He suggests that a way to do this is through the compensation structure to reward knowledge sharing – something that he understands the big consulting companies do.

Incentives provide a very strong driver for new ways of working and a change in behaviour. However they can be difficult to put in place as they need to integrate into company systems. They also have to be rigorously fair and universally applied, resulting in a high administrative burden. Further, the one occasion where an individual has been, or feels they have been, treated unfairly can result in discontent and adverse publicity. Sometimes existing incentives can be counter-productive to knowledge sharing as John Hardwick's experience with a US sales force demonstrates:

> They have national awards. Their incentives are a combination of meeting their sales target for the region, but also there is a national competition, if you're in the top 20 per cent of sales in the US then you get to go to Hawaii, or Europe or Australia, as an award. We actually identified that this competitiveness got in the way of Knowledge Transfer, when they did get hold of it, it was by stealth. When we interviewed the sales reps. 'how do you share your Good Practices?' the answer was 'why would we want to share our winning techniques and tactics, because we're all in competition with each other?' So we

did identify that as one of the barriers to Knowledge Management and Good Practice sharing, and they did change some of the incentives to make them more team oriented, so they did get more sharing within teams, if not across teams.

A more productive approach is to combine recognition and (small) rewards. Recognition is a visible and public reinforcement to individuals and teams that their behaviours model the new ways of working that the company desires from its staff. It can be at any level, from the individual to companywide. Recognition is often accompanied by some form of reward in order to make it more significant than a 'well done', and may include money or gifts which may or may not be made public (dependent on the company culture).

Verbal recognition from senior management and publicising knowledge sharing behaviours are powerful change enablers and are generally easy to carry out. Approaches that we have used at various times in our work with organisations to encourage knowledge sharing behaviours include citing examples of Good Practice and case studies at Town Hall meetings, publicly issuing small 'trophies' to role models, and incorporating articles in corporate communications. Examples of these approaches are also described by Goldstein and Schurr-Eisinger: they publicised interesting stories on their intranet, created an 'X-change' champion award (a modest cash sum) that anyone could give to someone who had been helpful in sharing their experience. These approaches all have a part to play in encouraging and sustaining the desired behaviours.

Tony Murabito had a similar experience of the powerfulness of senior management support at Cubist Pharmaceuticals in the US. The CEO led their Knowledge Management initiative from the top-down. Knowledge sharing was also 'incentivised' by being included in performance reviews across the whole organisation: from Research, into Clinical Development, Consumer and Public Affairs.

PERSONAL MOTIVATORS

The examples above are motivators that are put in place by the company as part of its KM strategy, but what of the individual, what motivation would there be for them to 'knowledge share' in its broadest sense, in their absence? David Gurteen's view is that if people understand that sharing their knowledge helps them do their jobs more effectively; helps them retain their jobs; helps them in their personal development and career progression; rewards them for getting things done (not for blind sharing); and brings more personal recognition, then knowledge sharing will become a reality. His reasons to share that should motivate people are:

- Knowledge is a perishable. Knowledge is increasingly short-lived. If you do not make use of your knowledge then it rapidly loses its value.

- If you do not make your knowledge productive then someone else with that same knowledge will. You can almost guarantee that whatever bright idea you have someone else somewhere in the organisation will be thinking along the same lines.

- By sharing your knowledge, you gain more then you lose. Sharing knowledge is a synergistic process – you get more out than you put in. If I share a product idea or a way of doing things with another person – then just the act of putting my idea into words or writing will help me shape and improve that idea. If I get into dialogue with the other person then I'll benefit from their knowledge, from their unique insights and improve my ideas further.

- To get most things done in an organisation today requires a collaborative effort. If you try to work alone you are likely to fail – you need not only the input from other people but their support and buy-in. Being open with them, sharing with them, helps you achieve your objectives.

Conclusion: Making the Change Happen

In this chapter we have discussed the six enablers in our KM Framework. Whilst we have described the different aspects of each of these enablers, the key is that they are all interlinked. For example, people will not change their behaviour unless they have the training and support to help them understand the new processes. Further, they will not be inclined to change unless they see that it is recognised and part of the way in which they are expected to work. However, KM ways of working will not become part of 'the way we do things around here' unless they are integrated into the company's performance system and ethos. That requires executive sponsorship which will only come if there is a vision for KM with clearly perceived benefits.

Of course, KM becoming 'the way we are doing things around here' is the goal, and then it can be forgotten that it was KM that got you there, as John Hardwick describes:

> *When you mention KM there's a rolling of the eyes, which is not a good reaction. We have to change that mindset. The only competitive advantage you can get these days is better use of your knowledge, and be quick to make decisions based on good knowledge.*

> *I think the tricky bit for KM (which is part of our change framework – Diagnose, Design, Implement. Embed, Grow) is the Embed and Grow phase. Some CoPs have now become the way they do business, and it's only when you stand back from, it is recognised that its genesis was Knowledge Management thinking and trying new ways of working. You need to get to that tipping point, or stickiness, instead of it being very conscious. It's like the feeling of writing with your left hand; it just becomes natural, and becomes an embedded process that you don't even talk about. That's the tricky bit. It's a bit like learning to drive. By the time you become a competent driver, you forget all the angst of learning to drive, and I think that you have to go through that very conscious 'front brain' approach to KM before you can get it embedded in your routine.*

For John Trigg, this is the ultimate aim: something that, if we get it right, we can just stand back and watch it grow. Goldstein and Schurr-Eisinger also stated it as their aim for Novartis back in 2005:

> *Our ultimate objective is to dissolve the Knowledge Management team because, at some point, knowledge will not be a project anymore; it will be the way we do work.*

For Michael Koenig, people will practice Knowledge Management because it is 'commonsensical':

> *People use information more intelligently, share it, communicate it more effectively and get it to the right people at the right time. At the end of the day it improves productivity, so what is there to argue about over that?*

So Michael finds it surprising that Knowledge Management has not been incorporated more into general management. If it were, there would be a dropping off in the use of Knowledge Management terminology in the literature. In fact, references in the literature are continuing to grow, suggesting that it is a topic that people still feel it necessary to explore and draw attention to. This brings us nicely to the next chapter, on the future of Knowledge Management.

Chapter 8
The Future of Knowledge Management

Introduction

This final chapter in our book explores how we anticipate Knowledge Management might continue to evolve, especially in the context of the Pharmaceutical Industry. Are Knowledge Management principles and techniques now integral to how pharma works, or have only some aspects been adopted (for example, After Action Reviews and other Learning Interventions, CoPs and so on)? Where are the opportunities and how can KM play a key role in the future in the changing pharmaceutical business models that we are witnessing, and in successful organisations in general?

Our own observations, and those of our interviewees, suggest the following main aspects, which we consider in two categories:

1.   Opportunities for Knowledge Management through the development of the Pharmaceutical Industry:

   •   the continuing evolution of the Pharmaceutical Industry;

   •   supporting collaborative knowledge sharing within and between organisations, whether or not defined as 'Open Innovation';

   •   new opportunities for generating knowledge from 'Big Data'.

2.   Opportunities relating to the development of Knowledge Management:

   •   the continuous 'reinvention' of Knowledge Management as a core competency within organisations;

- the close connection with Learning and Development and KM's intrinsic role in Learning Organisations;

- the use of social media both within organisations, and between organisations and their stakeholders, and cultural implications in the workplace.

We will take each of these in turn.

The Continuing Evolution of the Pharmaceutical Industry

We have not seen the end of the changes in the Pharmaceutical Industry. The downsizing and fragmentation that we described in Chapter 3 are still happening in a very dramatic way. The industry is reshaping: Burrill & Company's 2013 report on the Life Science Industry (Burrill & Company 2013) shows that over the previous three years the market capitalisation of 'Big Biotech' increased by 57 per cent against 'Big Pharma's' 17 per cent. This is driving acquisitions, the forging of new relationships and different ways of working together.

An example of these new relationships was when, in September 2012, ten of the largest companies announced (Pollack 2012) that they would collaborate to streamline clinical trials under a new non-profit organisation – TransCelerate BioPharma – specifically set up to co-ordinate the effort. Whilst companies have collaborated before in areas considered to be 'pre-competitive', this new initiative was said to be the largest so far, with a budget in the millions of dollars. Other companies, including smaller ones, would be able to join the ten founding companies, and non-profit organisations would also be included.

The announcement also said that the companies would be contributing personnel to work on the various projects involved, but they would only meet as necessary, rather than being based at TransCelerate's headquarters in Philadelphia. This kind of model has huge implications for Knowledge Management, for example, in clearly defining what knowledge from the parent companies does or does not get shared, in ensuring that insights from the TransCelerate projects are effectively disseminated back to the parent companies, and in determining what processes and technology are used for managing and sharing data, information and knowledge.

This example and the industry changes we described in Chapters 3 and 4, particularly relating to R&D, suggest that Knowledge Management will become more fragmented, and not necessarily described as KM, or driven centrally. Instead it will be a response to the needs of a project or business relationship for the capture, management and forward flow of knowledge. This means that many individuals will have responsibilities, which are recognisable as Knowledge Management but not labelled as such. This is not a new situation; people were managing knowledge long before KM was born. The challenge is to let people run with these local responsibilities whilst being part of an overall framework geared with the systems and processes that support decision making and the progression of a product through its lifecycle.

In Development and Manufacturing the implementation of ICH Q8, 9 and 10 that we described in Chapter 5 will necessitate a rigorous application of Knowledge Management to product knowledge. This will act as a counterbalance to the effects of cost-cutting, rationalisation and the drive for greater efficiency across the industry which have tended to push corporate efforts at KM to one side.

Supporting Collaborative Knowledge Sharing Between Organisations, Whether or Not Defined as 'Open Innovation'

As we have already mentioned, pharma has been going outside of its traditional borders for a while now, for example, through collaboration, outsourcing and alliances across the world.

Even in 2008 (Bartholomew 2008), Jim Murphy, of AMR Research, believed that a 'certain level of cynicism' about the term Knowledge Management had set in, and that it was really all about collaboration:

> *In the end, the highest order of Knowledge Management is collaboration.*
> *The goal is to enable people to work towards common goals, and*
> *Knowledge Management should ultimately contribute to that.*

As we write this book, 'Open Innovation' is very much the current phrase for collaborative working across organisational boundaries, business sectors and in Public Private Partnerships (PPPs). In fact Elisabeth Goodman has been working with Jackie Hunter, in her capacity as CEO of OI Pharma Partners, to deliver courses on Open Innovation to senior managers in pharma, and to support the development of various organisations' Open Innovation strategies.

This collaborative form of working makes the challenges and opportunities for sharing knowledge between the parties involved even more vivid than those within an organisation, and it also poses challenges for sharing, transitioning and protecting IP. For example, with pharma buying and selling companies and assets at various stages in their development, there is a need to know what assets and related information you had access to and when, at what stage of development, and how it relates to various collaborations so that IP (your own and that of your partners) can be protected appropriately. This is something that Michel Goldman, the CEO of IMI, understands well:

> Some people have a restricted vision of IP and IP rights. However most scientists as well as top executives realise the critical need to open the doors: having access to information outside of the usual landscape has a lot of value. In collaborative research industrialists agree to take some risk in sharing information because they realise that at the end of the day the balance will be positive.

This collaborative business model is also when the 'people', 'KM capability' and 'process' aspects of our KM Framework come into play.

CASE STUDY 1 – THE EMERGENCE OF A NEW BREED OF INTERMEDIARIES TO FACILITATE KNOWLEDGE SHARING WITHIN AND BETWEEN ORGANISATIONS

Janette Thomas has been working as an independent project manager in the Life Sciences since 2001. She works mainly with small biotech start-ups, often with only one to six full-time employees, and with a virtual network of associates and experts from academia, healthcare and pharmaceutical companies. It is a world that is becoming increasingly common with the fragmentation of the Pharmaceutical Industry.

Janette's role is broadly that of a facilitator to get a project started from the interpretation of the initial ideas, whether it is an academic or an inventor or someone with an idea about a business, to putting the processes in place for making it a reality. She does this by helping to build the relationships in the team, helping them to interpret the idea and putting some commercial practice into it, articulating their desired outcomes, drawing in the collaborators and expertise at the appropriate time, shaping their approach, steering them towards the development of project plans, sharing information from the literature which she thinks will be of value to them. It is a cross between science, business and sheer practicality that is heavily reliant on facilitation skills. You could say that her role is the modern day equivalent of the KM capability that originated within pharmaceutical companies.

Other aspects of Janette's work equate to some of the other Knowledge Management-related activities that we have described in this book. For example, she often manages the data and information generated within the company (technical and management documents, for example, for clinical trials, manufacturing or requiring management signature, meeting notes and so on), making sure that it is available in a central repository for all those involved, so that if anyone leaves, or if she is not available, the information is still available to others.

Because the organisations that Janette works with tend to be very young, or start-ups, she has not had the opportunity to help them review previous learnings for the work that she gets brought in to do. Rather, they expect her to come with knowledge of the relevant processes. Even where they have been around for a few years, they do not have any processes in place or real experience for how to share knowledge – it is very much all in their heads. So Janette has to pull this information from them, a key skill that she enjoys:

> It's pulling information from their heads. Obtaining information and explanations that are not obvious at all to provide, either because they are academics and know their subject so well, or because they have been so involved in their own business they don't know what they need to share with you. So it is a bit of an investigation: working out what they want to achieve and then making that happen for them.

CASE STUDY 2 – SERENDIPITOUS KNOWLEDGE SHARING FOR OPEN INNOVATION

In Chapter 7, we speak about the importance of 'serendipitous' knowledge sharing within organisations, and how the increasing shift to open plan and 'hot desking' environments is enabling more of this. In our third scenario in Chapter 4, on the evolution of collaborative working across organisations, Martino Picardo describes how serendipitous interaction is something that is also becoming commonplace between organisations at science parks such as the Stevenage BioScience Catalyst (in the UK) working in an Open Innovation environment.

We have come across different examples of how this serendipitous interaction is encouraged in our work with companies at science parks in and around Cambridge, UK: from simple provision of central catering and meeting facilities, regular provision of 'coffee and doughnuts', lunches for 'seniors', to facilitation of introductions between decision makers from different organisations.

New Opportunities for Generating New Knowledge From 'Big Data'

'Big Data' raises both challenges and opportunities for sharing data and information, and for generating new knowledge both within and between organisations. This reflects the 'content' component of our KM Framework.

In Chapter 4, we describe Lee Harland's work first in Pfizer, and then with IMI (in the Open PHACTS project) to facilitate the sharing and mining of data, and the generation of new knowledge. For Lee, Open PHACTS is very much a Knowledge Management project. It is one in which the team needs to address both the philosophy that this can be done, and real user cases of connecting external pre-clinical molecular biology and pharmacological data mostly in the public domain, with private data in a cloud computing environment. As Lee describes it:

> *It's a move away from building all-encompassing systems internally within pharmaceutical organisations, to enabling the wiring together of external and internal data via the cloud.*

This whole area is one that will continue to evolve so that, unlike other IMI projects, which have a definite end-point, the goal of the Open PHACTS project is to produce a long-term funding model. It is now official that Open PHACTS will continue as a non-profit charity akin to Lhasa Ltd, a non-profit industry consortium. The idea is that the long-term initiative would sell products or tools that various organisations, and especially small biotechs, could use, rather than having to develop their own.

Lee is taking this way of thinking even further, in a company, SciBite, which he founded to do just that. His scope is about understanding the drug discovery landscape: a version of what he did at Pfizer. His motivation is to provide medium and smaller worldwide pharma, small biotechs and academia with the opportunity to 'dabble' with data (data mining) in the Competitive Intelligence space, without the constraints of limited budgets. His inspiration is drawn from the book *Free* (Anderson 2010): providing a product for free that people are currently having to pay for, and then finding a way to make money from that. As Lee says:

> It's a bit like Google providing us with a free search engine, but actually gaining data from us in return: we are donating our time for this!

What SciBite does is to provide people with tools (like the one that Lee produced in Pfizer) using technology to do the data mining rather than people having to do this. There is a newsletter and a 'twitter-like' news feed of all the latest developments in key therapeutic areas. The data is curated using algorithms. By leveraging the latest text mining technology, SciBite is able to provide broad coverage at a fraction of the cost of traditional competitor intelligence tools. Lee wants to make it relevant to scientists and scientist-friendly, and all of this is now available. His whole approach is based around the changes in the Pharmaceutical Industry:

> The whole ecosystem is changing in that pharma's focus should be on how to put the pieces together: influence through standards and not try to build systems themselves, but rather concentrate on wiring things together. There are lots of small companies starting up outside pharma and creating small products. Pharma needs to concentrate on how to use these products.

Gene sequence data is another area with vast potential and challenges for Knowledge Management. It is one that Tony Murabito is still 'scratching his head about'. As he explains, HGS was one of the first companies to do gene sequencing. At the time that we spoke to Tony, HBS had 20 terabytes of 'unbelievable' data but there was not a lot of implicit knowledge attached to it – what the data meant. There was no process at the time that it was generated to capture the scientist's views on what the data could do, what functionality it could have or where it might be effective as a therapeutic. So HGS was looking for ways to imbue the data with knowledge either through computational paths or via external databases and partners. They were also bringing in some external advisors from IBM or Oracle to partner with them. As Tony says:

> It's still early days – but an area to crack to gain some value out of the realms of sequencing data we have at our fingertips. Even one or two leads would be rather profound for the company.

The Continuous 'Reinvention' of Knowledge Management as a Core Competency Within Organisations

As mentioned in Chapter 1, Knowledge Management has been around in its current form for about 20 years, and it looks like it is going to be sustained. Michael Koenig (Koenig 2012) makes a key point regarding KM in that, unlike some previous (maybe comparable) management topics (or fads!) of recent years, if the number of business articles published can assess the sustainability of the topic, Knowledge Management continues to grow (see Figure 8.1).

So where is Knowledge Management going, and why is there the perception that it is struggling to survive in the pharma industry and elsewhere? There are certain areas where the term has been discredited through failed initiatives or loss of interest, as other new initiatives and techniques come through, and as the corporate push that existed when KM first came along is no longer there. However we believe that the techniques established 15–20 years ago are still surviving, along with adapted and new tools and processes we describe throughout this chapter.

Sandra Ward believes that KM is regularly not so much reinvented as rediscovered! KM is often a low priority when mergers and acquisitions occur – it can disappear very quickly during these events even though its value at this point is potentially tremendous. Which experts do we retain? Which Discovery programmes are most critical? Then, as the new company solidifies it can re-emerge – often as the problems of work duplication, difficulties of finding experts and locating information reveal themselves again. The new companies in the industry also discover the KM need as they increase in size.

> *Everyone knows the term and it's as if different groups in companies discover 'we need to do something because we're wasting our knowledge and expertise'. KM may also happen in pockets; this is still relevant although it creates less corporate advantage.*

In the 1990s the Pharmaceutical Industry was prominent in the KM space with corporate initiatives at Astra Zeneca, GW, Novartis, Pfizer Roche and SmithKline Beecham. Does the focus on process and efficiency mean that KM has been embedded in the industry? GSK's annual report for 2012 would seem to confirm this: 'At the core of our business model is the use of knowledge and development of intellectual property.'

Below are the graphs for three hot management topics (or fads) of recent years

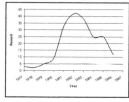

Quality Circles, 1977–1986
Source: Abrahamson,1996

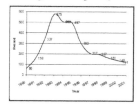

Total Quality Management, 1990–2001
Source: Ponzi & Koenig, 2002

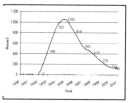

Business Process Reengineering, 1990–2001
Source: Ponzi & Koenig, 2002

KM looks dramatically different:

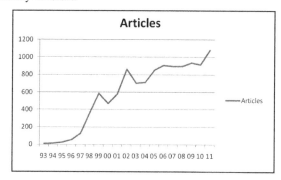

This graphs charts the number of articles in the business literature with the phrase 'Knowledge Management' in the title.

If we chart the number of articles in the business literature with the phrase 'Knowledge Management' or the abbreviation 'KM' in the title, we get the chart below, with an order of magnitude more literature:

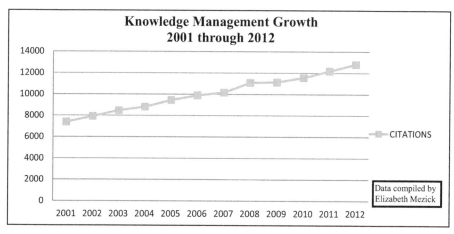

Figure 8.1 **Articles published on Knowledge Management compared with other business initiatives**

As Sandra points out, the whole business of teams sharing knowledge is still critically important. In her experience, people who are leading project development and development projects have, quite naturally, decided that they need to network in order to exchange their experience and learn from one another as they take their projects forward. The need for Competitor Intelligence is also a well-understood activity, dependent on KM, and Sandra cannot imagine that it does not exist in every organisation.

Finally, as Sandra says, there are some activities that intrinsically require some form of Knowledge Management and Knowledge Transfer to happen. These include sharing knowledge whenever there is a change in staff, either operationally or on project teams, getting new staff up to speed rapidly, ensuring that all the necessary knowledge is available for decision support, and when dealing with problems or issues, and for innovation, and reflecting and capturing knowledge from diverse and substantial pieces of work for future use and sharing with others.

Many of the people that we spoke to, whether actual KM practitioners or individuals who have come across aspects of Knowledge Management in their work, still value the likes of Learning Interventions and CoPs for active sharing of insights and experiences – the 'people'-related components of our KM Framework. As we have described, the 'content' component of our framework is also still continuing to evolve. And people with the required capabilities are developing their roles in the interface between organisations, as well as within a range of departments not explicitly defined as KM ones.

Maybe we are still a long way from seeing Knowledge Management established as a recognised discipline or competency in companies, but we should still ask the question 'Why not?' Matthew Loxton compares Knowledge as a discipline to Finance:

> You can run a firm without a CFO and you will still be 'doing finance', just not very well, and the same holds for knowledge – you can do it haphuzardly, but you will be basically letting random chance run 80 per cent of your assets.

Whilst there is a clear argument for Knowledge Management as a discipline, there is, and to an extent always has been, an issue with the label 'Knowledge Management'. It usually requires explanation, does not fit with our traditional concept of a management discipline and means different things to different people. There is also a certain weariness or even an issue of credibility with the term as John Hardwick described in Chapter 7. John Davies believes that the Knowledge Management term will disappear. He says that it is very difficult to manage knowledge, that thought leaders are unanimous in this and that in ten year's time people will not be talking about 'knowledge' anything, but about ways of working: a perspective that reinforces our message throughout this book. Other trends that John describes are:

> Knowledge practitioners will become very adept at organisational development techniques such as use of open spaces, appreciative enquiry, small and large group techniques, idea generation, innovation (with and without technology) – more sophisticated than using post-it notes and theoretically guided (in the style of David Gurteen's Knowledge Cafés).

> KM has come from libraries and will go back to libraries. CKOs are now often running libraries. People are using multiple tools. Google replacing library roles for searching.

The Close Connection With Learning and Development and Knowledge Management's Intrinsic Role in Learning Organisations

John Riddell has carried out a significant amount of work on linking Learning and Development to Knowledge Management, which presents several opportunities for KM. This work covered how the focus for most Learning and Development strategies – the individual – can be linked to the development of organisational capability in key business areas through Knowledge Management. By connecting people through KM techniques such as CoPs, competency in a topic or subject area can be more rapidly developed (see quote in Chapter 3) than by working in isolation. Peer collaboration in this environment can further develop existing expertise. This provides a vehicle for the development of competency in key areas at a business level leading to improved performance, as illustrated in Figure 8.2.

The development of KM in an organisation enables performance to be improved beyond the aggregate of what individuals might achieve in a specific field. In the Engineering sector, Arup have inserted behaviours such as those described into their competency profiles and implemented a KM strategy that supports the exchange of knowledge and expertise (Larkman n.d.).

Developing Organisational Capability

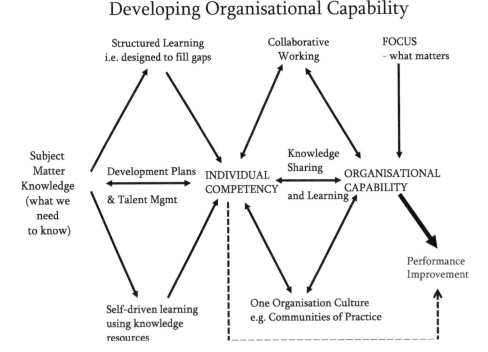

Figure 8.2   Integrating Knowledge Management and learning to develop organisational capability

This integration should start at induction, to plug people into the desired culture, and go right through to ensuring retirees and leavers have passed on their key knowledge. In between, the KM tools that are getting the most attention are those that promote capturing and sharing learning for operational, project and general business development: After Action Reviews; Learning Before, During and After; CoPs. Some organisations are using coaches such as Helen Chapman to facilitate this, others are using new style intermediaries such as Janette Thomas, and yet others are still recruiting Knowledge Managers.

For Helen, the group coaching or team coaching that she does is all about knowledge sharing:

> It's either helping individuals to realise what they know and learn from their own experiences in a way they perhaps have not thought about doing; or it's about helping teams to do that; or it's about helping groups to do that. Companies that want to be more Learning Organisation-orientated and more innovative are going the 'let's operate with more of a coaching culture route'.

Using Social Media Both Within Organisations, and Between Organisations and Their Stakeholders

The idea of using something like social media for enhancing knowledge sharing between individuals is not a new one. In 2006, before many of the tools that we now currently use were even around, Thomas W. Parsons et al. submitted a conference paper on a study within the Pharmaceutical Industry (Parsons, Jackson & Dawson 2006), which, amongst other things, advocated the formation of communities around drug projects and the provision of tools to encourage collaboration across the organisation, and the capture of 'minutiae' from these communities. They were not sure what these tools should be, although they listed blogs and wikis as possibilities, as well as groupware document-based systems (a current example of which would be SharePoint).

Social media, like it or not, is with us and will continue to be with us albeit in an ever-changing form. A new generation (variously referred to as Generations Y, Z, A and the Millennials) are growing up communicating in a different way. John Riddell's wife is part of a large family and her mother is finding that after being the knowledge hub for decades, news is now travelling faster around the family through Facebook than via her regular phone call cycle!

Elisabeth Goodman recently wrote an article on how Twitter could be an intrinsic component of any individual's 'Knowledge Management toolbox' (Goodman 2012), enabling individuals to both 'push' and 'pull' information, to find a vast range of people with multiple interests and specialities, to create Communities of Interest, and to learn before, during and after.

There have been a number of obstacles to the implementation of social media in business: lack of familiarity and expertise at a management level, concerns over confidentiality and risks to the organisation's reputation, the wide range of products and social media services to choose from, and a preference for simply waiting to see what happens with the pioneers before going with what works. There is a conflict between social media's core use for socialising and the 'time is money' ethos of the business day. However, organisations are increasingly recognising that social media also bring some real benefits, for example by engaging staff in problem solving and innovation, and by engaging external stakeholders with their brands, and with product and service development. Business needs a purposeful strategy and an approach which benefits both the organisation and the individual. To this end, many organisations have developed or are developing guidelines and policies to balance all of these potentially conflicting requirements. In our snapshot we look at scenarios for using social media internally and for linking externally with stakeholders.

USING SOCIAL MEDIA WITHIN ORGANISATIONS

Within organisations, companies are now experimenting with tools like Yammer, as a sort of Twitter within their firewall. They are using it as a general communication alternative to e-mail, for serendipitous knowledge sharing across departmental boundaries, but also in more formal ways for sourcing ideas and addressing problems, for example in project teams. The traction for Yammer is definitely growing and in the long term will become integrated with SharePoint (Clark 2013). One interviewee describes how putting knowledge that he gained onto Yammer helped make a connection across the organisation:

> *A UK site was doing work on Raman Spectroscopy and trying to make a decision on a new hand-held spectrometer, which I picked up through a conversation with them. I put it on Yammer and a USA site saw it and flagged up that they were doing the same. I've now brought the two of them together to see how they can work it collaboratively.*

In a recent webinar (Dellow 2013), Larry Cannell, a Research Director at Gartner, suggested that whilst Yammer should primarily be a tool for social networking and communities, and SharePoint should be used for document libraries, customised websites and information tracking, there is a potentially increasing overlap between the two, for instance for user profiles, blogs and wikis. All these have Knowledge Management-related implications within an organisation.

In addition, John Davies refers to 'presence' technology: where employees can call up people's names on a system and see their availability. Similarly, SharePoint contains information about people and gives them the confidence to contact each other and be relatively informal. He compares these technologies to original attempts with 'yellow pages' systems in organisations that had mixed results. For John, these 'presence' systems are like 'taking a cork out of a bottle'.

And new ways of using technology to foster networking are continuously being invented. In a recent HBR blog (Hewlett 2013), Sylvia Ann Hewlett describes Boehringer Ingelheim's new 'lunchtime roulette'. Individuals wishing to participate use a new in-house application to randomly match them with another employee for lunch. At the time the blog was written, more than 350 people, including the CEO, were taking part and, as we would expect, this approach not only 'produces unexpected pairings but often sparks unexpected conversations'.

USING SOCIAL MEDIA WITH STAKEHOLDERS

Stephen Clulow believes that social media has huge potential for pharma but that companies are not really looking at it from a strategic perspective – how it could be used to support innovation and growth strategies. The Pharmaceutical Industry works in a highly regulated and sometimes litigious environment. He thinks this can prevent the adoption of social media in healthcare, but that people can be trained to use the tools responsibly and effectively.

However, it is a medium that is gaining increasing traction between pharmaceutical organisations and their stakeholders. Many companies now have formal accounts on Twitter and LinkedIn, where they share news and jobs and, more importantly from a knowledge sharing perspective, pick up what their followers are saying that might affect any aspect of their business.

In Chapter 3 we described how Tony Murabito and his team have been using social media to engage his company's external community in knowledge sharing around specific diseases and their therapy. He has also been working with a non-profit group in New York, the T1D Exchange, to develop a concept around Diabetes disease management in a social media forum: to share practices, do monitoring, refer people to physicians and give ratings to physicians. It is being sponsored by the Helmsley Foundation and is proving to be an interesting way to blend technology, science and all the social aspects into one forum.

As Sandra Ward points out, the increasing demand for transparency about what companies are doing also links to the vogue in social media and the emergence of new types of knowledge capital and patient intelligence – knowledge resources that need ongoing and immediate monitoring and analysis. She has noted that pharma companies are now taking social intelligence very seriously. She has observed small KM/Information Management (IM) teams, often in R&D, taking the initiative to explore how text analytics can be used to track social media content to identify:

- What are patients saying about our products?

- What are they saying about the therapeutic areas that we have selected as R&D targets – what are their unmet needs?

- How do we use that to influence our discovery and development programmes, and also our sales and marketing activity?

SOME FURTHER THOUGHTS ON SOCIAL MEDIA

Going back again to Parsons et al.'s 2006 paper, their research not only suggested that social software (as they called it) would be particularly important in the interface between discovery and clinical departments within organisations, but it also highlighted the potential role of these tools in the then relatively new model of in-licensing compounds for Discovery, and in the use of public clinical data in-house. In both situations the authors found that internal employees tended to revalidate the existing data and information, rather than capturing the external know-how and disseminating it throughout the acquiring organisation. Whilst some collaborations with external sources did occur, they tended to be unstructured and relied on more traditional media such as e-mail, face-to-face interactions and the phone.

Microsoft's acquisition of Yammer will undoubtedly bring the application into the mainstream of business software and together with SharePoint will provide powerful vehicles for knowledge sharing and collaboration. The generations for which these tools are second nature are already in, or coming into, the workplace, and those of us in the older generations are spread along the adoption curve. However, the enablers that we set out in Chapter 7 still apply if the tools are to be productive. We are seeing examples across industry of systems being made available without governance, training, facilitation, support, and most of all – without a clear demonstration of their value. Usage is frequently variable and the result counter-productive. Full understanding and engagement is needed in order to avoid a gravitation to the 90-9-1 that exists on the internet, where 1 per cent of users create the majority of the content, 9 per cent comment or tag, and 90 per cent just consume information (T-Systems Multimedia Solutions n.d.).

However we are in a transitional phase, much as when e-mail was first being introduced, and the opportunity is there. As Tony Murabito says:

> Social media gives us ways to connect people, practitioners and experts in ways that were not possible before. Now we're at the dawn of the next technology age and the facilitation of Knowledge Management.

One of the challenges is how these new tools will sit alongside e-mail, to which much of industry seems addicted. Can we manage new ways to communicate and share when the most knowledgeable and experienced people have to spend a significant portion of their day dealing with e-mails that range from critical to superfluous? E-mail has proved its value over the last three decades as a secure means to communicate one-to-one or one-to-few. However, its success also means that it can be used inappropriately, such that it becomes a nuisance or an actual barrier to effective communication through other more traditional routes.

What is key for those involved with Knowledge Management is the role social media can play in collaboration, and how it then integrates, or even replaces, existing approaches. A big concern of many in this technological age is retaining the art of conversation, the richest form of Knowledge Exchange. Sherry Tuckle is a psychologist who highlights how people are losing the opportunity for conversations because they are now 'alone with their devices'. She highlights this change in this anecdote (Tuckle 2012):

> I spend the summers at a cottage on Cape Cod, and for decades I walked the same dunes that Thoreau once walked. Not too long ago, people walked with their heads up, looking at the water, the sky, the sand and at one another, talking. Now they often walk with their heads down, typing. Even when they are with friends, partners, children, everyone is on their own devices.

Conclusion: Knowledge Management Will Simply Continue Because There Will Always be New Knowledge to Deal With!

In a recent NetIKX seminar (Goodman, Knowledge Management: past, present and future – notes on a NetIKX seminar 2013) the consensus amongst the delegates was that KM would continue to be around, although it might not necessarily be called Knowledge Management. Certainly everything that we have heard, seen and experienced supports that. The pace of organisational change, the associated high turnover of staff and the seemingly exponential growth of knowledge all pose challenges to anyone engaged in channelling our world of knowledge into pharmaceutical processes, services and products. In addition, the regulated environment, latterly with ICH Q8, 9 and 10 requires us to have systems and processes to manage and maintain that knowledge.

As Sandra Ward points out, the diversity of the areas surrounding the core pharma business such as sustainability, biodiversity, carbon footprints and safety all add to that exponential growth of knowledge.

Michel Goldman suggests that pharma itself has a role in identifying ways in which it can make better use of KM practices:

> *More and more, KM will be as important as medical research: because if we keep generating data without integrating them through new KM approaches, we will continue to lose time, energy, money. It's critical for Pharma to develop a new kind of research: how to take advantage of the new KM tools to create new knowledge. To create new knowledge you don't necessarily need to accumulate more data. Perhaps just by using knowledge more efficiently we will derive new information.*

When all is said and done, we believe that the KM principles and practices, as represented by our Framework, and whether explicitly referred to as Knowledge Management or not, will continue to provide strong support for 'channelling' the time, energy and money associated with the continuously evolving world of knowledge in the Pharmaceutical Industry. Putting time, effort and energy into Knowledge Management is an investment in a better informed, more integrated and unified way of working, enabling better decision making and, ultimately, improved performance and outcomes for this important industry.

Appendix
The Interviewees
(with Bios where provided)

David Alderson

Maryrose Brennan

Helen Chapman

Helen Chapman is the Managing Director of Pelican Coaching and Development and a qualified and accredited psychological coach and trainer. She is passionate about helping leaders and teams to be more effective and resilient in creative and innovative ways. Helen has more than 22 years' experience in large multinational organisations working in management and leadership roles in functions such as Research, Development, IT, Finance, Information and Knowledge management. She started her life as a bench chemist at Nicholas Laboratories, before moving to ICI and then GSK. At GSK she led multinational project and programme teams, a consultancy team focusing on driving organisational change and complex international groups before deciding to set up her own coaching and development company.

Stephen Clulow

Dr Stephen Clulow has 20 years' experience in biotechs and pharmaceutical companies in the UK, Europe and USA. This includes: lead isolation, optimisation and late-stage compound profiling for small molecules and biopharmaceuticals; leading interdisciplinary teams to generate business cases for new products; implementing IT systems for clinical data management, biomarker data mining and knowledge management.

In 2012 Stephen founded the Open Innovation consultancy Action for Innovation Limited. They enable healthcare companies to solve challenges, enhance their capabilities and fill product pipelines through internal innovation projects and external partnering.

David A. Cunningham

David graduated as a Pharmacist and had an extensive career in the Pharmaceutical Industry with Glaxo and latterly GSK. He manufactured medicinal products covering a wide range of dose forms, both steriles and non-steriles. He also manufactured pharmaceutical actives. Later in his career, he led a team providing technical support and services to the group sites and contractors.

He then spent five years with Medicines and Healthcare products Regulatory Agency (MHRA) as a Good Manufacturing Practice (GMP) Inspector. Since April 2009, David has been an independent consultant performing gap analysis audits prior to regulatory inspections, site audits on behalf of customers, generating remedial action plans after regulatory inspections and providing validation and quality systems training.

John Davies

John Davies is the Head of Business Consultancy in the Public Sector Software Division at IDOX PLC where his responsibilities include developing the business consulting and innovation capability and looking to provide strategic and process consulting across the public sector using in-house expertise and a network of associates. He is an Organisational Consultant and Interim Manager who combines business content with specialist Knowledge, Information and Records Management experience gained in the public and private sectors both in the UK and overseas.

Steven Friend

Michel Goldman

Michel Goldman, Executive Director of IMI, builds and promotes networks of innovation, in close collaboration with all stakeholders involved in pharmaceutical R&D. IMI supports the launch and successful continuation of collaborative programmes to foster research and development activities on more effective and safer therapies for patients across Europe.

Michel is Professor of Immunology at the Faculty of Medicine of the Université Libre de Bruxelles, Belgium. His achievements in the fields of immune-mediated disorders and immune-based biotherapies resulted in more than 400 articles.

In 2000, Michel Goldman received the Joseph Maisin Prize, a major award for clinical sciences delivered by the Belgian Fund for Scientific Research, and he held the Spinoza chair at the University of Amsterdam in 2001. He was recognised as an ISI Highly Cited Scientist by the Thomson Institute for Scientific Information in 2006. Michel Goldman was awarded the degree of Doctor Honoris Causa of the Université Lille II, France in 2007.

Lee Harland

Lee received his BSc. (Biochemistry) from the University of Manchester, UK and PhD (Epigenetics & Gene Therapy) from the University of London, UK. Lee has over 15 years' experience leading informatics within major Pharma. His experience spans data management, integration & warehousing, vocabulary & ontology, text mining, competitor intelligence, knowledge and information management, data mining, bio- & chemo-informatics and software development. He is currently the CTO of the Open PHACTS project (http:// openphacts.org) and CEO of SciBite Limited (http://scibite.com), two novel drug discovery intelligence portals.

John Hardwick

Jacqueline Hunter

Professor Jacqueline Hunter CBE, is currently Chief Executive of OI Pharma Partners Limited. She has an extensive record in developing and running global centres of excellence in pharmaceutical research and is a leader in the application of open innovation principles to Life Sciences R&D. In 2010 Jackie received a CBE for Services to the Pharmaceutical Industry and was presented with a Women of Achievement in Science, Engineering & Technology award.

She is a Fellow of the British Pharmacological Society and holds a personal Chair at St George's Hospital Medical School.

Michael E.D. Koenig

Michael E.D. Koenig is Professor at Long Island University, and is the former and founding Dean of the College of Information and Computer Science at LIU. His career has included both academic positions and senior management positions in the information industry, including Manager of Information Services for Pfizer Research, and VP positions at the Institute for Scientific Information, Swets and Zeitlinger, and Tradenet Inc., and Dean and Professor at Dominican University.

Michael obtained his PhD in information science from Drexel University, an MBA in Mathematical Methods and Computers and an MS in Library and Information Science from the University of Chicago, and his undergraduate degree in Psychology and Physics is from Yale University. A Fulbright Scholar in Argentina, he is the author of more than 100 peer-reviewed scholarly publications, the co-editor of three monographs on the subject of KM published for the American Society for Information Science and Technology, including 'Knowledge Management: What Works and What Doesn't', a member of the editorial board of more than a dozen journals, and a past president of the International Society for Scientometrics and Informetrics. He is also the recipient of a Jason Farradane award for 'Outstanding Work in the Information Field'.

John Larkin

John was the CIO of Millipore, a $800m global high tech manufacturer, for nine years. Millipore was an early adopter of global processes and shared services enabled by an ERP platform.

He was RVP at Oracle Consulting for six years where he was responsible for applications and technology practices including the North East Applications area practice. He is a Co-Founder of TPP with a focus on strategy, governance, alignment and architecture.

Matthew Loxton

Matthew is a certified Knowledge Management practitioner with extensive international experience in putting knowledge to work in achieving organisational goals, and has served in senior global KM roles in the USA and Australia. Matthew holds a Master's degree in Knowledge Management from the University of Canberra, and is a peer reviewer for the international *Journal of Knowledge Management Research & Practice*. *Pro bono* roles have included KM and IT Governance work with the Queensland Emergency Medicine Research Foundation (QEMRF) and the St Andrew's Medical Research Institute (SAMI). Matthew currently works as a Senior Analyst for Knowledge Management at Whitney, Bradley, & Brown, contracting to the Veterans Healthcare Administration, and blogs on Knowledge Management and Organisational Learning.

Arnold Mabbett

Ann Marie Martin

Ann is responsible for the Knowledge Management Collaborative Projects at the Innovative Medicines Initiative, that is, projects with a focus on document management, data pooling and data processing infrastructure. In recent years, she has been researching the potential of open source collaborations in both statistical programming and patient initiatives working with a patient organisation dedicated to research in generalised or DYT1 Dystonia.

Ann has held various management positions in the Pharmaceutical Industry including Global Head of Biostatistics for UCB Pharma, Global Section Head of Statistical Programming for Novartis and Global Head Statistical Programming Operations, Standards and CDISC Implementation at UCB Pharma, giving her a broad knowledge of drug development and extensive international experience with Europe, the US and India.

Ann holds a Master's degree in Sociology and Statistics from the London School of Economics and Political Science, UK.

Tony Murabito

Anthony (Tony) S. Murabito joined HGS in September 2011 as Vice President and Chief Information Officer. Prior to joining HGS, Tony spent over eight years as Chief Information Officer at Cubist Pharmaceuticals, where he directed a complex IT environment including numerous development and architecture projects in support of commercial, research, business and collaboration partners. From 2001 to 2003, Mr Murabito was Vice President, Information Technology and Corporate Services for Transkaryotic Therapies where in, addition to Information Technology, he was responsible for facilities, site construction, office and lab services. He was previously with SmithKline Beecham for almost 20 years, with responsibility for global R&D information systems. Mr Murabito is a Registered Pharmacist and a member of the Pennsylvania and New Jersey Society of Health System Pharmacists. He received his BS in Pharmacy from Philadelphia College of Pharmacy and Science and an MS in Health Administration and Information Sciences from Widener University. He is a member of the New England CIO Biotech Forum and the TIBCO CIO Advisory Board.

Phil Nethercote

Stephanie North

Stephanie is the Director of Allyl Consulting Ltd. She is an enthusiastic and accomplished information management professional with a passion for delivering solutions and benefits to business leaders and scientists and demonstrating strong leadership, communication and influencing skills. Stephanie has over 20 years' proven track record with a blue chip pharmaceutical company. Her specialities include information management, strategy and requirements analysis, chemical information and facilitating knowledge transfer between organisations engaged in outsourcing and collaborations. Stephanie has expertise in the management of information for collaborations and outsourcing and in the integration of scientific information from mergers and acquisitions.

Mark Perrott

Mark is a Life Sciences Consultant at Foresight Group International, AG. He has more than 18 years' business process improvement and change management expertise across multiple areas of pharmaceutical R&D where he has improved processes and assured lasting change in clients and employers from the largest pharmacos to small biotech start-ups.

Mark's expertise includes programme and project management, change management and effective implementation, and he has deep subject matter expertise in clinical development and pharmacovigilance.

Martino Picardo

Martino is the first CEO of the Stevenage Bioscience Catalyst, an ambitious concept to develop an Incubator and Accelerator, followed by a world class Science Park for the Life Sciences sector. Martino has a PhD in Biochemistry from Cardiff University and spent four years at Baylor College of Medicine, Houston, TX in cardiovascular research. Martino joined Amersham International in 1991 and subsequently went on to manage the R&D Technology Transfer Group, based in Cardiff and developing high throughput screening technologies for the pharmaceutical sector. Following the merger of Amersham with Pharmacia Biotech, Martino became the Science Director for the Cardiff site, Martino then became a Business Manager for Manchester Biotech Ltd and subsequently Manchester Innovation Ltd in June 1999. When the Universities of Manchester and UMIST merged, he became Managing Director of University of Manchester Innovation Centre (UMIC) and Manchester Incubator Company Ltd (MICL) and is also currently a Board member of UK Business Incubation (UKBI). Martino is also acting Chairman for a start-up company, sri Forensics Ltd and has previously been on the Board of Cartesian Technologies, Bionow Steering Committee and was also a non-executive Director for Queen Mary Bioenterprise Ltd (2009–Aug 2010). Martino is now also a Board member of the Hertfordshire Local Enterprise Partnership (LEP).

Hedley Rees

Janette Thomas

Dr Janette Thomas is a senior executive working in the pharmaceutical and biotechnology industries since finishing her postdoctoral fellowship in Biotechnology and Biochemistry at the University of Cambridge in 1994. Janette has managed large international development projects for 'large pharma', created Biotechnology companies, and managed 'virtual' development teams for small organisations to develop business plans, licensing deals, and R&D programmes, all in a variety of indications and stages of development. Janette is Director of her own consultancy company, AccentBio Ltd, and she volunteers as Finance Director for the Pharmaceutical Industry Project Management Group (PIPMG). Janette has a PhD from the University of Leicester and her most recent qualification is a Diploma in Company Direction from the Institute of Directors. (www.accentbio.com, www.pipmg.com)

John Trigg

John Trigg is Founder and Director of phaseFour Informatics, a UK-based consultancy specialising in the Electronic Laboratory Notebooks and laboratory integration. He has extensive experience working in the field of R&D data, information and knowledge management, including ten years' experience of the world's first enterprise-level implementation of an Electronic Lab Notebook in the Eastman Kodak Company. John is author of a number of publications on Electronic Laboratory Notebooks and Knowledge Management in the Laboratory and has presented papers and run workshops at conferences in the UK, Ireland, mainland Europe, USA and Australia. John is also the founder of The Integrated Lab website. He was the recipient of the 2000 International LIMS Award and is currently the Chairman of the Automation and Analytical Management Group of the Royal Society of Chemistry and an Advisory Board Member of the Institute for Laboratory Automation.

Frank van Amsterdam

Frank van Amsterdam originally graduated as a Medicinal Chemist at the Free University of Amsterdam and then obtained a cum laude PhD in Pharmacology at the University of Groningen. He started working at Glaxo in Verona as head of a Biochemistry lab, became director of Scientific Computing at GlaxoWellcome, of Informatics and Knowledge Management at GSK and finally of Information Management, also at GSK. He led a global programme to increase findability of R&D information, R&D Search, and built a tool to manage standardised dictionaries, mandatorily used across all of R&D-IT. These tools were closely integrated to build 'GSK Search', the GSK internal 'Google', and became the starting point for a Master Data Management initiative in Clinical Trial Management.

With the transition in 2010 of the GSK R&D Centre in Verona to Aptuit, a globally operating CRO, Frank became Director of Market Intelligence/ Information Management collecting external 'intelligence' for Sales and Operations, but also organising internal information in a centralised knowledge base to assist Sales informing (potential) clients in a complete and consistent way about Aptuit's global service offerings.

Since June 2013 Frank has been working for Cognizant Technology Solutions in the Life Sciences division in the UK as Associate Director, Information and Data Services.

Sandra Ward

As Director of Information Services (UK) for Glaxo Wellcome R&D, Sandra Ward was actively involved with the company's initial Knowledge Management activities, targeted at making explicit knowledge and experts easy to find. As Head of Consultancy and Training for TFPL Ltd, thought leaders in KM in the 2000s, Sandra led initiatives to ensure that organisations capitalised on their knowledge and experience through strategies that blended people, content and techniques with business needs. She co-authored the 2001 PJB report: 'Mobilising Knowledge: The Pharmaceutical Industry Approach', as well as working with Novartis, Cambridge Antibody Technology (now MedImmune), Astra Zeneca and Merck Serono, amongst others. As an independent consultant, Sandra now trains in knowledge transfer techniques, undertakes knowledge audits and KM reviews, and partners on KM strategy development.

Alison Zartarian

Alison Zartarian has worked in the field of project management for over 14 years; firstly in the nuclear medicine industry managing new product development, IS and engineering projects, then subsequently in the pharmaceuticals industry. Her current role is to improve the level of project management capability across R&D in a large, global pharmaceutical company and is managing a change programme to increase the level of knowledge sharing amongst project teams. Alison has a PhD in Physical Chemistry from the University of Edinburgh and is a PMI-certified Project Management Professional.

Bibliography

Anderson, Chris. *Free: How today's smartest businesses profit by giving something for nothing.* London: Random House Business, 2010.

Bartholomew, Doug. 'Brain Rein – as AstraZeneca and Baxter have discovered, knowledge management technologies can harness a companys collective (and global) intellect'. *Pharmaceutical Manufacturing,* 6 August 2008.

Bawden, David, and Elizabeth Orna. 'Information and knowledge management'. In *Pharmaceutical and Medicines Information Management: Principles and Practice,* by David Bawden, Alan Judd and Andrew Robson, 38–59. Elsevier Health Sciences, 2001.

BBSRC. 'Dynamic Gastric Model'. 28 February 2013. http://www.bbsrc.ac.uk/ news/research-technologies/2013/130228-n-commercial-future-for-model-gut.aspx (accessed 12 March 2013).

Burrill & Company. 'Big Biotech outpaces Big Pharma'. 16 April 2013. http:// www.burrillandco.com/content/news/PR-BIO-2013–4-16–13-final.pdf (accessed 25 July 2013).

Cambridge Consultants. 'India: Driving world pharmaceuticals by 2030?' 2013. www.cambridgeconsultants.com/2013-india-workshop-report (accessed 12 March 2013).

Campbell, Stephen J., Anna Gaulton, John Marshall, Dmitri Bichko, Sid Martin, Cory Brouwer, and Lee Harland. 'Visualizing the drug target landscape'. *Drug Discovery Today,* 15 (1/2), January 2010: 3–15.

Center for Army Lessons Learned. n.d. http://usacac.army.mil/cac2/call/index. asp (accessed 31 October 2013).

Clark, Chris. 'SharePoint Social vs. Yammer – with user interfaces, looks can kill'. 15 August 2013. http://www.cmswire.com/cms/social-business/ sharepoint-social-vs-yammer-with-user-interfaces-looks-can-kill-022131.php.

Clemmons Rumizen, Melissie. *The Complete Idiot's Guide to Knowledge Management*. Madison: CWL Publishing, 2002

Collison, Chris, and Geoff Parcell. *Learning to Fly*. Second Edition (First Edition 2001). Chichester: Capstone Publishing, 2004.

Dellow, James. 'Ripple Effect Group'. 'Gartner: Yammer or SharePoint? The choice is still unclear.' 15 March 2013. http://rippleffectgroup. com/2013/03/15/gartner-yammer-or-sharepoint-the-choice-is-still-unclear/ (accessed 1 April 2013).

Duhon, Bryant. 'It's all in our heads'. *Inform*, September 1998, p. 12.

e-business W@tch. 'Knowledge Management solutions driving drug discovery from Aureus Pharma (France)'. *e-business W@tch*. July 2005. http://ec.europa. eu/enterprise/archives/e-business-watch/studies/case_studies/documents/ Case%20Studies%202005/CS_SR04_Pharma_6-Aureus.pdf (accessed 21 October 2013).

'Eudralex Volume 4'. 'European Commission Health and Consumers Directorate General'. 6 September 2012. http://ec.europa.eu/health/files/ eudralex/vol-4/vol4-chap1_2012–06_en.pdf (accessed 15 March 2013).

Gladwell, Malcolm. *The Tipping Point*. New York: Little, Brown & Company, 2000.

Goncalves, Alexis. 'Driving innovation through networks'. Presentation made at the ASQ World Conference on Quality and Improvement, Anaheim, CA. 21 May 2012. http://www.slideshare.net/goncalvesalexis/driving-innovation-through-networks (accessed 13 January 2013).

Goodman, Elisabeth C. 'Records management as an information management discipline – a case study from SmithKline Beecham Pharmaceuticals'. *International Journal of Information Management*, 14(2), 1994: 134–143.

Goodman, Elisabeth. 'Knowledge Management: past, present and future – notes on a NetIKX seminar'. *NetIKX*. 2013 http://elisabethgoodman.wordpress. com/2013/03/22/knowledge-management-past-present-and-future-notes-on-a-netikx-seminar-netikx60/ (accessed 1 May 2014)

—— . 'Putting Twitter in your knowledge management toolbox'. *Freepint*. 5 April 2012. http://web.freepint.com/go/sub/article/68492 (accessed 5 April 2012).

Gurteen, David. 'Creating a knowledge sharing culture'. *Knowledge Management Magazine*, 2(5), February 1999.

— . 'Regional Gurteen Community Cafés'. n.d. http://www.gurteen.com/gurteen/gurteen.nsf/id/kcafes (accessed 29 January 2013).

Hardy, Barry. 'Knowledge Management in pharmaceutical manufacturing – optimising efficencies in knowledge transfer'. *The Ferryman,* 30 June 2005. http://barryhardy.blogs.com/theferryman/2005/06/knowledge_manag.html (accessed 21 March 2013).

Harland, Lee, Christopher Larminie, Susanna-Assunta Sansone, Sorana Popa, Scott Marshall, Michael Braxenthaler, Michael Cantor, Wendy Fisell, Mark J. Foster, Enoch Huang, Andreas Matern, Mark Musen, Jasmin Saric, Ted Slater, Jabe Wilson, Nick Lynch, John Wise, and Ian Dix. 'Empowering industrial research with shared biomedical vocabularies'. *Drug Discovery Today,* September 2011: 1–8.

Hewlett, Sylvia Ann. 'A new way to network inside your company'. *HBR blog network,* 8 January 2013.

Hunt, Vivian, Nigel Manson, and Paul Morgan. 'A wake-up call for Big Pharma'. *McKinsey & Company.* December 2011. http://www.mckinsey.com/insights/health_systems_and_services/a_wake-up_call_for_big_pharma (accessed 20 June 2012).

IBM. 'http://scaledinnovation.com/innovation/publications/2009–08-ibm.pdf'. IBM Case Study. 21 June 2010.

ICH Harmonised Tripartite Guideline. 'ICH Q10 Finalised Guideline'. 4 June 2008. http://www.ich.org/fileadmin/Public_Web_Site/ICH_Products/Guidelines/Quality/Q10/Step4/Q10_Guideline.pdf (15 March 2013).

— . 'Pharmaceutical Development Q8 (current step 4 version)'. August 2009. http://www.ich.org/fileadmin/Public_Web_Site/ICH_Products/Guidelines/Quality/Q8_R1/Step4/Q8_R2_Guideline.pdf (accessed 15 March 2013).

IMI. 'Innovative Medicines Initiative'. n.d. http://www.imi.europa.eu/ (accessed 7 August 2012).

Katzenbach, Jon R, Ilon Steffen, and Caroline Kronley. 'Cultural change that sticks. Start with what's already working'. *Harvard Business Review,* July–August, 2012: 100–117.

Kleiner, Art, and George Roth. 'How to make experience your company's best teacher'. *Harvard Business Review*, September/October 1997.

Koenig, Michael. 'What is KM? Knowledge Management explained'. *KM World*, 2012.

Kwiecien, Stan. 'Best practice replication – the evolution of KM at Ford Motor Company'. *Inside Knowledge*, 10 October 2001.

Larkman, Debra. 'Integrating formal and informal learning; linking knowledge management and L&D'. Ark Group. n.d. http://www.ark-group.com/audio/Training/formalinformal/formalinformal.html (accessed 10 July 2013).

Leavit, Paige M. 'The role of Knowledge Management in new drug development'. *APQC*. n.d. http://www.providersedge.com/docs/km_articles/Role_of_KM_in_New_Drug_Development.pdf (accessed 16 April 2013).

McDermott, Richard, William M Snyder, and Etienne Wenger. *Cultivating Communities of Practice*. Boston, MA: Harvard Business Press, 2002.

Merck. 'Our Values'. Merck.com. n.d. http://www.merck.com/about/our-values/home.html (accessed 13 October 2013).

Milton, Nick. 'Survey – the size of KM teams'. Knoco Stories. 3 June 2011. http://www.nickmilton.com/2011/06/survey-size-of-km-teams.html (29 August 2013).

Moss-Kanter, Rosabeth. *The Change Masters – Corporate Entrepreneurs at Work*. New York: Simon & Schuster, 1983.

Newman, Victor. *The Knowledge Activist's Handbook*. Chichester: Capstone Publishing Ltd, 2002.

Nonaka, Ikujiro, and Hirotaka Takeuchi. *The Knowledge Creating Company: How Japanese companies create the dynamics of innovation*. New York: Oxford University Press, 1995.

O'Dell, Carla. 'The Executive's Role in Knowledge Management', 32 and 39–41. Houston, TX: APQC, 2004.

One Nucleus. n.d. http://www.onenucleus.com/ (accessed 3 March 2013).

Parsons, Thomas W, Thomas W Jackson, and Ray Dawson. 'What drives pharmaceutical innovation and knowledge exchange? A study supporting the use of Knowledge Management within the pharmaceutical industry'. *OLKC 2006 Conference at the University of Warwick, Coventry on 20–22 March 2006.*

Patterson, Kerry, Joseph Grenny, David Maxfield, Ron McMillan, and Al Switzler. *Influencer: The power to change anything.* New York: McGraw Hill, 2008.

Pfizer. 'Pfizer's commitments for a healthier world'. Pfizer.com. 14 Oct 2009. http://www.pfizer.com/files/about/pfizer_commitments.pdf (accessed 29 March 2013).

Pollack, Andrew. 'Drug makers join efforts in research'. *The New York Times*, 19 September 2012.

Schurr-Eisinge, Sabine, and Maurice Goldstein. 'Member spotlight: Knowledge sharing for drug development at Novartis'. *Working Knowledge, the newsletter of the Babson Working Knowledge Research Centre.* Summer 2005: 10–11.

Snowden, Dave. 'Blog'. Cognitive Edge. 24 September 2009. http://cognitive-edge.com/blog/entry/3185/defining-km/ (accessed 5 May 2012).

Sorani, Marco D., Ward A. Ortmann, Erik P. Bierwagen, and Timothy W. Behrens. 'Clinical and biological data integration for biomarker discovery'. *Drug Discovery Today*, 15 (17/18), 2010: 741–748.

T-Systems Multimedia Solutions. 'The Wikipedia Myth–Enterprise 2.0 Knowledge Management'. SlideShare. n.d. http://www.slideshare.net/TSystemsMMS/the-wikipedia-myth-enterprise-20-knowledge-management (accessed 5 September 2013).

Tuckle, Sherry. 'The flight from conversation'. *New York Times,* 21 April 2012. http://www.nytimes.com/2012/04/22/opinion/sunday/the-flight-from-conversation.html?pagewanted=1&_r=1 (accessed 28 July 2013).

UCB. 'Vision'. UCB.com. n.d. http://www.ucb.com/about-ucb/vision (accessed 29 March 2013).

Index